CHARITY AFFILIATION: UNCOVERING A NEW KEY VARIABLE FOR CAUSE-RELATED MARKETING

By

Carolanne Kuntz Azan, D.B.A.

Author	Carolanne Kuntz Azan, D.B.A., Tampa, FL
Publisher	DBC Publishing, Virginia Beach / Richmond, VA
ISBN	ISBN-13: 978-0692871812 ISBN-10: 0692871810
Cover Art	Copyright 2017©; Carolanne Kuntz Azan, D.B.A.

Author: You may contact the author with questions, comments, or continuing research inquiries at: dr.carolannekuntz@yahoo.com

TABLE OF CONTENTS

Table of Contents **3**
   List Of Tables 7
   Table Of Figures 8
Acknowledgements and Dedications **9**
Foreword **11**
Abstract **13**
Chapter One: Introduction **15**
   Problem Background 25
   Purpose of the Study 33
   Research Question 34
   Hypothesis 34
   Limitations of the Study 34
   Delimitations of the Study 38
   Significance of the Study 39
   Definitions of Terms 42
Chapter Two: Review of the Literature **49**
   Introduction 49
   Corporate Social Responsibility 50
   Cause-Related Marketing 54
      Campaigns 56
      Partnerships 60
      Cause-Related Marketing Sponsors 66
      Charitable Non-Profit Organizations (Charities) 68
      Sponsor's Cause-Related Marketing Campaign
      Product 74
      Cause-Related Marketing Donation Practices 77
      Ethical Dilemmas 81
      Globalization 85

Cause-Related Marketing Marketing Strategy and Segmentation.. 89
Consumers in General 93
Baby Boomers as Consumers 99
Millennials as Consumers 102
Generation Z as Consumers 105
Social Media... 107
Affiliation 110
Employees 112
Volunteers 113
Donors.. 119
Beneficiaries.. 122
Guiding Principles/Personal Rules...................... 124
Purchase Preference 125
Brands.. 131
Economic Factors 134
Emotions 136
Price 137
Quality 139
Demographic Attributes 139
Limited Research 141

Chapter Three: Methodology...............143
Research Design 145
Research Model.. 146
Research Question 149
Hypothesis 149
Sampling and Respondents..................................... 150
Population and Sample... 150
Sampling Method 151
Response Rate 154
Respondent Profile... 155
Instrumentation 157
Age Qualifying Question 158
Variables 158
Independent Variable... 159
Dependent Variable 161
Demographic Variables.. 162
Survey Measurements 163
Respondent Demographics.................................. 164
Respondent Affiliation 167

Cause-Related Marketing Campaigns................. 167
Purchase Preference for CRM Campaign Products
.... 169
Methodological Assumptions and Limitations...... 169
Procedures 171
    Feedback from Panel of Experts........................... 173
    Survey Administration 179
    Statistical Tests... 180
Data Processing and Analysis 181
Assumptions Underlying Principal Component
Analysis (PCA).. 183

Chapter Four: Results.....................................187
Restatement of the Purpose 187
    Research Question 187
    Research Findings 188
Survey Response Data Analysis 189
    Respondent Demographic Profile 189
    Affiliation.. 193
    Respondent Affiliation 194
    Immediate Family/Close Friend Affiliation.............. 197
    Purchase Preference 200
Hypothesis Testing 203
    Individual Question Regressions............................ 204
    Hypothesis Testing Linear Regression Models...... 206
Summary of Results 210
Supplemental Statistical Analysis 212
Summary of Supplemental Data.......................... 213

**Chapter Five: Summary, Recommendations, and
Conclusions...215**
Summary of Study 215
    Statement of Problem 216
    Purpose of Study.. 217
    Review of the Literature 217
    Methodology.. 219
Findings 221
    Limitations and Delimitations of Findings.............. 223
    Implications and Implementations for Practice....... 225
    Charities 226
    Sponsors 227

Consumers...229
Recommendations for Future Research.............. 230
Contributions to Academic Literature Stream 233
Conclusions 233
References 237
Appendices 245
Appendix A 247
Survey Instrument..247
Appendix B 249
Survey Instrument Feedback from Panel of Experts
....249
Index 253
Curriculum Vitae..261
Author Bio...277
Connect to the Author 279
Book Reviews 280
About the Book...281

LIST OF TABLES

Table 1: Individualism and Collectivism Domains Assessed in Individualism-Collectivism Scales .87
Table 2: Organizations and Number of Potential Participants 151
Table 3: Paired Samples Correlations 175
Table 4: Paired Samples Statistics 176
Table 5: Paired Samples Test 177
Table 6: Respondent Demographics 191
Table 7: Respondent Affiliation 195
Table 8: Immediate Family / Close Friend Affiliation
.... 198
Table 9: Summary of Affiliation 200
Table 10: Likely to Make CRM Purchase 201
Table 11:- Likely to Purchase CRM vs. non-CRM
Product 203
Table 12: Regression Model: Benefit Predicting Purchase Preferences 205
Table 13: Summary of Linear Regression Models: Composite Affiliation Predicting CRM Purchase
.... 207
Table 14: Summary of Linear Regression Models: Composite Affiliation Predicting CRM vs. Non-CRM Purchase 208
Table 15: Summary of Linear Regression Models: Affiliation Predicting the Composite Purchase Preference Score 209

TABLE OF FIGURES

Figure 1 - Consumer Decision-Making Model 98
Figure 2 - Research Model for Affiliation (Kuntz-Azan, 2016)...148
Figure 3 - Research Model for Affiliation and Purchase Preference (Kuntz-Azan, 2016).......149
Figure 4 - The sequence of the research study events. 182

ACKNOWLEDGEMENTS AND DEDICATIONS

The many years of research, regarding Charity Affiliation were all encompassing, but also a labor of love. It was very important to me to conduct research that would contribute to filling a gap for marketers in non-profit organizations. This was not a solitary effort, and I will forever be grateful to everyone who assisted me with their expert opinions, feedback and research that was conducted for this book. Without the collaboration of everyone mentioned, completing this work would not have been possible.

I would like to thank my chair and committee members for guiding me through the dissertation process. I want to especially thank my friend, mentor and colleague, Dr. Sherri Kae for her expertise in survey development and for her collaboration on the survey instrument that was used in this study. A significant part of this book reflects her knowledge and expertise in cause-related marketing and quantitative analysis, as Dr. Kae spent months editing this manuscript with me. I look forward to the day when I am working with my own graduate students, as I have been so blessed to have had such a wonderful role model.

To my family and friends. Thank you so much for your love and support over the last few years, when all my time was spent with my nose in a book. To my wonderful and supportive husband Alex, and my late in-laws, Dr. & Mrs. Luis Azan, for reasons that are too many to mention, and incredibly difficult to put into words. To my parents, Howard and Susan Kuntz. You brought me up with the inherent values of giving back to the community, helping strangers and being kind to animals. You have made all my past dreams come true, and you will always be the reason my future dreams are possible.

I especially want to thank all the employees, volunteers and donors who dedicate their time to charitable non-profit organizations. You are sincerely changing the world with your caring spirit and humanity. A portion of the proceeds from this book will be donated to animal rescue charities in my beloved 'second home,' St. Augustine, Florida.

"Keep your thinking cap on and keep going!"

Carolanne Kuntz Azan, D.B.A.

FOREWORD

The majority of the information in this book is derived from the author's doctoral dissertation entitled, *Charity Affiliation and Consumer Purchase Preference for Cause-Related Marketing (CRM) Campaign Products*© (2016). The format has been changed and this book should not be used as a dissertation outline.

'Charity Affiliation,' and the measurement for affiliation are new to the academic literature stream, and will provide greater specification in charitable relationships and affiliation.

The research conducted for this book indicates the presence of a relationship between charity affiliation and consumer purchase preference for cause-related marketing (CRM) campaign products. This research suggests a new way to target markets that could assist with the creation of product lines which may be more appealing based on demographics.

Consumers may face better decision-making information when evaluating a CRM purchase if sponsors and charities both engage in more transparent activities and choices for CRM campaigns. Both charities and sponsors may want to adjust their market segmentation and targeting practices based on the findings of this research. This research suggests that CRM is extremely sensitive to demographics. A better understanding of purchase preference based upon the strength of consumers' affiliation may support or alter current market segmentation and the targeted marketing efforts of both CRM sponsors and charities engaged in CRM, or in their daily mission to find more volunteers and donors. Charities, sponsors and consumers are all impacted by the results of this study in many other ways, which are further discussed in the book.

It is essential to note, the affiliation of both respondent and immediate family and close friends is important in an individual's decision to purchase a CRM product; however, *there are many other factors that contribute to their decision that may be revealed from the additional questions that were included in the survey, not used to test the dissertation hypothesis.* Further research and analysis is being conducted, and a second book regarding those factors is forthcoming.

ABSTRACT

The purpose of this study was to investigate the prevalence and strength of a consumer's affiliation with a charity and to quantify the strength of the relationship between consumer affiliation and their purchase preference for cause-related marketing campaign products. This research was a quantitative study utilizing an on-line survey for data collection presented to employees from three for-profit organizations and employees and volunteers from two charities.

Hypothesis testing revealed that respondent employment at a charity, donations to a charity and volunteering at a charity, which are measures of affiliation, were found to be significantly related to Cause-Related Marketing (CRM) purchase preference for both the likelihood of making a CRM purchase and likelihood of making a CRM vs. a Non-CRM purchase.

Hypothesis testing also revealed immediate family members/close friend's affiliation was significantly related to CRM purchase preference for both the likelihood of making a CRM purchase and the likelihood of making a CRM versus a non-CRM purchase.

Respondent affiliation and the immediate family members/close friend's affiliation together was significantly related to the composite CRM purchase preference score, which revealed as individual affiliation increased, purchase preference increased.

Thus, the alternative hypothesis, indicating the presence of a relationship between affiliation and purchase preference was accepted.

Keywords: cause-related marketing, charity affiliation, purchase preference

CHAPTER ONE:

INTRODUCTION

Organizations have been donating money and products to those in need as far back as when mom and pop stores were populating a marketplace absent of large factories and retail stores. It was only in the last several years (2000-2017) that organizations are identifying themselves as socially responsible and engaging in Corporate Social Responsibility (CSR), specifically with Cause-Related Marketing (CRM). Consumers are beginning to hold organizations accountable for their CSR practices, "and view their purchasing power as influential over company behavior" (Mohr, Webb, & Harris, 2001, p. 45). CSR includes both avoiding harm and doing good. Overall, CSR supports doing business in a way that maintains or improves both the customer's and society's well-being (Mohr et al., 2001).

Cause-Related Marketing is based on a relationship between a CRM sponsor and a charity. Non-profit organizations and charities were not one and the same. Forester (2013) clarified, "While all charities are nonprofits, not all nonprofits are charities" (www.score.org). There are varying kinds of charities. Organizations such as homeowner's associations and clubs were formed as mutually beneficial non-profit organizations. Whereas charities were formed for benefiting the public. Charities file different types of tax returns and were eligible for a 501(c)(3) tax-exempt status due to their charitable mission. Charities may also receive tax-deductible donations (Forester, 2013).

Cause-related marketing was first utilized in a 1981 CRM campaign by American Express in support of the restoration of the Statue of Liberty (Kelley, 1991). The concept of CRM was introduced by Varadarajan and Menon in their 1988 article wherein the concept of CRM was defined, CRM characteristics illustrated and the benefits of CRM to organizations and causes discussed. Cause-related marketing was "a marketing program that attempts to achieve two goals – improving corporate performance and helping worthy causes by connecting fund raising for the benefit of a cause to the purchase of a firm's products" (Varadarajan & Menon, 1988, p. 58). The purpose of CRM was, "to capitalize on a firm's social engagement initiatives to achieve a positive return on a firm's social investment" (Liston-Heyes & Liu, 2013, p. 243).

Cause-related marketing provided significant benefits to both CRM sponsors and charities, as well as to consumers. "Firms benefit because the campaigns are profit-motivated. That is, donations are made based on consumer behavior, which is most often exercised by purchasing the sponsoring company's product" (Grau & Folse, 2007, p. 20). Charites value the CRM relationship: "Much of the non-profit's operations are based on donations, and the CRM campaigns improve their ability to continue with their mission by increasing resources and awareness" (Grau & Folse, 2007, p. 20). The consumer connection to charities gained attention, as well: "Consumers find cause-driven partnerships a socially responsible means to contribute to the community. In addition, some consumers appear to enjoy the process of participating in campaigns" (Grau

& Folse, 2007, p. 20).

Examples of CRM campaigns, were such as Yoplait Yogurt and New Balance with the Susan G. Komen Foundation, Kay Jewelers with St. Jude Research Children's Hospital, Wendy's and the Dave Thomas Foundation for Adoption, Starbucks and the Oprah Winfrey Leadership Academy Foundation, Cumberland Farms and the ALS Association, and Unilever partnered with Direct Relief. "Despite increasing trends of cause-related marketing and corporate social responsibility in general, the idea of being socially responsible, beyond the formal scope of business activities, still is relatively new" (Vanhamme, Lindgreen, Reast, & van Popering, 2012, p. 264).

Firms became more conscientious about … their public images (Szykman, Bloom, & Blazing, 2004). The Corporate Social Responsibility Index Study (2010) stated, "company's reputations are affected by public perceptions of performance related to citizenship, governance, and workplace practices. The 2010 study's results show companies are improving socially responsible practices; the public is more aware and interested in these efforts" (Boston

College, Carroll School of Management, 2010).

Consumers may have favorable attitudes toward companies that supported a cause. Grau and Folse (2007) wrote, "Some consumers experience a close identification with a cause or company, and appear to be drawn to a campaign because they consider the cause to be relevant to them" (p. 21). However, consumers may be suspicious of the motives of the CRM sponsor. Mohr, Webb, and Harris (2001) suggested, "The public has less confidence in big business than other institutions such as the military, the police, public schools, and newspapers" (p. 45). One counter-thought was organizations practicing CRM were thinking more about themselves than the charity to which they are aligned. Some consumers felt the CRM sponsor's motives were focused on increasing profitability and market share, rather than moral reasons. "As consumer skepticism increases, firms have begun to realize that consumers also expect greater corporate social responsibility" (Demetriou, Papasolomou, & Vrontis, 2010, p. 266).

Consequently, CRM organizations may have wanted to reevaluate the value their CRM partner brought to their CRM mission.

> *CRM is a strategic partnership that should make sense as a long-term commitment. The cause needs to provide both a national and local connection to help drive sales. If there is no opportunity to move a product, the marketer won't be motivated to make a financial commitment to the cause" (Thomas, 2005, p. 71).*

Often, organizations selected their CRM partner for reasons other than improving the organization's bottom line or attracting the highest number of consumers possible in such a relationship. "A marketer who wants to adopt a CRM program must be aware that well-implemented and well-promoted CRM programs have the potential to bring enormous benefits to the partnership" (Demetriou et al., 2010, p. 267).

Market segmentation was the process of aggregating individuals along similar characteristics that pertain to the use, consumption, and/or benefits of a product. Target marketing was the process of selecting the market segments that were most attractive to the company which included accessibility, profitability, and growth potential (Strauss & Frost, 2014). Moreover, effective segmenting and target marketing by levels of high affiliation could impact the entire strategy for a CRM sponsor choosing to partner with a charity. CRM sponsors may more closely evaluate the attributes and size of the charity. A CRM sponsor may withdraw from a current charity partnership and select a more suitable one. If respondents measured high on the various components of affiliation, and measured high on purchase preference, CRM sponsors may have asked the charity associated with their CRM mission to provide databases of charity employees, volunteers, beneficiaries, and donors. Such information enhanced their marketing efforts, increased the efficiency of market segmentation and targeting, and improved their proceeds by selling more products. In turn, this improved the benefit amount to the charity.

In addition, "The 21st Century is witnessing an unprecedented expansion of volunteering and service, domestically and internationally, both in numbers of volunteers and sponsoring organizations"

(Sherraden, Lough, & McBride, 2008, p. 395). Retired Baby Boomers and other older adults may be motivated to volunteer to give back and provide stability and daily activity within their lives (Sherraden et al., 2008). Baby Boomers were born between 1946 and 1964 and upon becoming adults, they took over the consumer market one year at a time. Baby Boomers now are 29% of the workforce (2015; www.pewresearch.org); however, they were well into their move into retirement, leaving their career jobs vacant. Baby Boomers who were living on Social Security and pensions were, first, at a stage of life where their needs had changed and, second, limited in the amount of money they could have earned while maintaining their Social Security and pensions. Those two lifestyle changes resulted in Baby Boomers with extra time and very different needs. One need of Baby Boomers was to give back and they were doing so by volunteering their time to charities.

Now, "Millennials exhibit their own forms of participation, volunteering at a higher rate than other generations" (Castillo, 2015, p. 4). Over the course of time as they became older, their affiliations could become stronger and their value for giving back most likely will be passed onto their children. Consequently, millennial adults were very interested in volunteering and giving to charities they valued. The growth of this generation cannot be ignored; the values they held dear to their hearts, were giving of their time and their money.

Consequently, volunteers and those with other affiliations to charities may be a fast-growing segment. Understanding the behavior of consumers with strong and weak affiliations with charities could have significantly impacted target marketing and market segmentation for CRM efforts. Anderson and Kotler (2008) stated, "A marketing manager for a non-profit organization must begin with an understanding of the target audience behavior, because the organization's success depends on it" (p. 116). Those with strong affiliations with charities are likely to better understand the needs of charities and their beneficiaries. Such consumers may have also emotionally connected with a specific charity or charities in general; more so than those consumers with weak or no affiliation with charities. "Engagement and involvement with charities are a factor in predicting future intention to donate. This may be due to the association between engagement and identification" (Baruch & Sang, 2012, p. 808).

Furthermore, factors or attributes which enhanced purchase preference were going to be of utmost importance to both CRM sponsors and charities. Oftentimes, a purchase decision was more than a choice of products, manufacturers, retailer, CRM sponsors or price, leaving the final decision based on emotion. An emotional decision may be well thought out and reasoned or it may have been an automatic response to an emotional trigger. "Interest in emotions related to product and brand strategy is not surprising, given the hedonic benefits of an emotional reaction connection" (Franzak, Makarem, & Jae, 2014, p. 18).

Although the shift to a CRM marketing strategy was slow, it was prominent in the landscape of competitive industries and strategic groups both nationally and internationally. As stated by Strahilevitz and Myers (1998), "Linking purchases with charitable donations can be an effective marketing tool" (p. 434). Nevertheless, a complacent attitude was lethal in today's global environment.

However, implementing and executing a new marketing strategy was known to be the most time consuming and laborious stage of a marketing plan. Unfortunately, as with any new strategy, adoption was often quick and not well thought out, thus negatively impacting the outcomes.

According to Liston-Heyes and Liu (2013), "While there is considerable work on CRM from a corporate angle, very little has been done from a non-profit perspective, particularly in terms of developing a conceptual and theoretical understanding of the strategies available to non-profit managers" (p. 1974). Determining the most effective way to segment and identify target markets for cause-related marketing required an understanding of the role of affiliation and its relationship to purchasing preference.

Problem Background

The problem facing CRM sponsors adopting a CRM strategy was the tendency to add the intangible benefit of giving to the original marketing plan for the CRM campaign product, but ignored the value of the intangible attributes felt by consumers when they purchased a CRM campaign product.

Perhaps one reason it had been difficult to coax marketers into putting more effort into CRM was that, "We have been forewarned that social marketing is no easy task" (Goldberg, 1995, p. 347). Incorporating the value of the intangible attributes felt by consumers when they purchase a CRM campaign product provided a significant advantage to marketers. One intangible attribute would have been the 'feel good' value of giving to a needy charity. Eikenberry (2013) pointed out, "In 2010, 41% of Cone's survey respondents had bought a product associated with a cause over the past year, up from 20% of respondents in 1993" (p. 290).

At the time of this research study, the tendency to segment the market for CRM campaign products was based on the attributes of consumers or those consumers likely to purchase in that product category. However, the attribute of affiliation with a charity may have produced a better segmentation plan and required advertising and marketing efforts different from those used at the time of this research study. Although affiliation may not be the single attribute to best attract consumers to CRM campaign products, it may have been a very important attribute depending on the size and focus of the charity. This train of thought brings to light the determination of who was the consumer of CRM campaign products – those consumers who needed or wanted the CRM campaign product for simply the product attributes or those consumers who primarily wanted to support the charity with little care about the product itself, those consumers who switched brands to support the charity when purchasing the product, or any of these combinations?

Consumers often purchased things they do not want or need for a variety of reasons, but when the reason was to feel good for 'giving,' the question becomes why did 'giving' motivate a consumer to switch brands, purchase a product that he or she did not need or want, or to have given simply to support the charity? In addition, why was 'giving' a motivator in CRM decisions? Vallerand (2012) defined motivation as, "the hypothetical construct used to describe the internal and/or external forces that produce the initiation, direction, intensity and persistence of behavior" (p. 45). When applied to CRM, the origin and strength of the 'feel good' value in consumers was often ignored in the segmentation portion of the marketing plan. In other words, why did some consumers readily purchase CRM campaign products whereas others did not, and who and where were the consumers that had a higher motivation to purchase CRM campaign products?

Arnett, German, and Hunted (2003) asserted, "Identity theory posits that people have several 'identities,' that is, self-conceptions or self-definitions in their lives" (p. 89). There were direct positive psychological effects of volunteering and donor satisfaction. Some of these effects were stronger relationships, development of support teams, a sense of meaning in life, and helping to maintain self-identity (Arnett et al., 2003). Franzak, Makarem, and Jae (2014) contended, "Theories of affect in psychology research have demonstrated that different emotions are associated with different behavioral responses" (p. 18). Philanthropic psychology was an emerging field based on what motivates donors to give, and much of that motivation was from identity saliency. Moreover, "Engagement and involvement with charities is a factor in predicting future intention to donate. This may be due to the association between engagement and identification" (Baruch & Sang, 2012, p. 808). Vis-à-vis, the intangible 'feel good' attribute may have come from a sense of belonging, meaning, and fulfillment. "In the past decade, consumer research has moved from a sole focus on cognitive decision-making to recognizing the importance of the emotional component of consumer behavior" (Franzak et al., 2014, p. 18).

Choi and Kim (2011) professed, "Social bonds and close human interactions are also the basis of charitable-giving behavior. Donors tend to base their donation decisions on their involvement in relationships, and giving tends to reinforce the social bond" (p. 590). Thus, the ill-conceived CRM marketing plan ignored the power of and motivation associated with the 'feel good' attribute of giving and ignored the usefulness of segmenting the market based on consumers who had a higher motivation to purchase a CRM campaign product, regardless of the product, price, or CRM donation practice. Shu-Pei (1990) explained, "There still lacks sophisticated delineation to explicate the antecedents and consequences of positive motivational attribution. Without such delineation, the brand marketer may rely on intuition instead of strategic thinking when planning and implementing CRM" (p. 650). Relying on intuition instead of strategic planning could be a costly mistake for marketers. Care should be made regarding the differentiation of positive motivational attributes that could take planning and time. An efficacious marketing strategy was vital; identifying an effective and unique approach was a challenge.

When achieving, and sustaining a competitive advantage, companies paid attention to differentiation. Deac and Stanescu (2014) stressed the need for "a company to identify those ways through which it can truly differentiate, highlighting specialization in a specific activity" (p. 45). There were many different types of consumer behaviors. Some common shopping and spending traits had been shown to impact loyalty to a brand or to a specific store. This has been found to be true in older clients who were more likely not to purchase a substitute brand if their preferred brand was not available (Foxall, 1978). Frequent shoppers had lower brand loyalty and those shoppers who socialized with their neighbors showed higher brand loyalty (Foxall, 1978). Consumers that showed a high level of brand engagement had been labeled as "influencers," and it had been suggested they were known to recommend their favorite products and brands, especially in our current tech-savvy and connected society.

Spending traits also included consumers' connections to CSR, along with consumer confidence and its link to consumer expectations regarding perceptions of economic conditions. It was suggested that, "a substantial, viable, and identifiable market segment exists that considers a company's level of social responsibility in its purchase decisions" (Mohr, Webb, & Harris, 2001, p. 69). An understanding of consumer expectations of CSR should be noted when creating CRM campaigns. Kwan and Cotsomitis (2004) stated, "Consumer confidence reflects consumer perceptions of future economic trends. As such, confidence indices constituted a convenient and useful tool for predicting future household spending" (p. 136). Economic trends included purchasing power, inflation, and recession. When income was high relative to the cost of living, consumers were likely to spend more money on wants rather than needs (Lamb, Hair, & McDaniel, 2013). The way consumers perceived economic trends and how that related to their purchasing behavior was vitally important to marketers. There were numerous strategic drivers for an organization that included "market type, sales marketing method, and market segmenting" (Thompson, Strickland, & Gamble, 2008, p. 129).

Furthermore, it was vitally important for organizations to understand how to elicit behaviors that related to purchase preference, including a thorough understanding of the consumer decision process. The consumer decision process directly intersected between the marketing strategy and the outcomes (Lamb et al., 2013). Understanding consumer decision-making, buying behavior, and the confidence levels of consumers directly affects marketers and all involved in aligning with a partner and developing CRM campaigns. Organizations adopting a CRM mission will find it crucial to evaluate all aspects of consumers who were purchasing CRM campaign products to ensure their relationship with a charity provided both parties with the most beneficial results. A better understanding of purchase preferences based upon the strength of a consumer's affiliations may support or alter current market segmentation and targeted marketing efforts.

Purpose of the Study

The purpose of this research study was:

1. To investigate the prevalence and strength of a consumer's affiliation with a charity.
2. To quantify the strength of the relationship between consumer affiliation and their purchase preference for cause-related marketing campaign products.

For this research, consumer affiliation was defined as the "consumer and the consumer's immediate family and close friends who has/have, at the time of this research study, or in the past been an employee of, a volunteer with, a beneficiary of, or a donor (product or money) to a charity." A better understanding of purchase preference based upon the strength of consumers' affiliation may have supported or altered current market segmentation and the targeted marketing efforts of CRM sponsors engaged in CRM.

Research Question

RQ1: What is the relationship between charity affiliation and purchase preference for cause-related marketing campaign products?

Hypothesis

H_1: There is a relationship between charity affiliation and purchase preference for cause-related marketing campaign products.

H_0: There is not a relationship between charity affiliation and purchase preference for cause-related marketing campaign products.

Limitations of the Study

For this study, quantitative research methods were utilized to investigate and explore the relationship between consumer affiliation and purchase preference. A quantitative approach was chosen due to its many advantages. This research study was exploratory and utilizes a new variable: affiliation; consequently, a quantitative method was needed to statistically analyze the reliability and validity of affiliation

Limitations of the quantitative survey methodology utilized for this research study included generalizability, response rate, number of observations for affiliation, inability to contact non-respondents, time restraints, and potential flaws within on-line data collection methods.

It is not uncommon for generalizability to be a limitation of exploratory research such as this study. The convenience sample, limited geographic location of the respondents, type of charities, and sample size greatly impacted the ability of this study to be generalized to the public. It was expected the results would be generalizable to the culture of other similarly structured organizations in the Tampa Bay area.

The sample consisted of two charitable non-profit organizations and three for-profit organizations located in the Tampa Bay area, which did not represent all charities nor all for-profit organizations. Therefore, within the parameters of the research design there are certain limitations on generalizability.

Response rate was related to validity. There were eight measures of affiliation in the study: (1) respondent as an employee, (2) a volunteer, (3) a beneficiary, and (4) a donor, and the respondent's recall of their (5) immediate family members and close friends as employees, (6) volunteers, (7) beneficiaries, and (8) donors. A low response rate made the statistical analysis of validity difficult, if not impossible; particularly if sufficient responses for each of the eight affiliation categories are not received. Limited observations for the various dynamics of affiliation would, in turn, limit the statistical analysis of this new variable (affiliation) and limit testing validity.

Anonymity and confidentiality for respondents inherently restricted the researcher from sending personal email reminders. Reminders had to be sent to all respondents and could be sent only to those who have not yet responded. Consequently, this limitation may have negatively impacted response rate, validity and generalizability. Limitations also included inability to meet time constraints. The organizations may have restricted access for survey administration and distribution to a limited period. Such constraints may have limited the respondents' ability to complete the survey at a time convenient for them. If an organization's response rates were low, the organization may or may not have allowed another distribution of the survey.

Lastly, the potential flaws within on-line data collection methods included the need for a large sample size, low interaction with respondents, and the severity of nonresponse bias. To mitigate these potential flaws, the sum of both the non-profit and the three for-profit organizations sent the survey link equated to 2,914 potential respondents. Since there was no interaction between the researcher and the respondent, the Survey Monkey survey instrument may have possibly included colorful category headers that were visually stimulating. To alleviate non-response bias, charitable non-profit and for-profit organizations were chosen to collect the data to avoid over-representation and under-representation of the population.

Delimitations of the Study

This study had delimitations which had to be taken into account. Delimitations imposed to narrow the scope and define the boundaries of the study included surveying only those who lived and worked in the Tampa Bay area, the selected methodology, and purchase preference. The sample consisted of men and women, 18 years of age, or older who live, work and volunteer in the Tampa Bay area. A quantitative approach was selected rather than the bifurcated methodology. As stressed by Creswell, Klassen, Clark, and Smith (2010), "Because multiple forms of data are being collected and analyzed, mixed methods research requires extensive time and resources to carry out the multiple steps involved in mixed-methods research, including the time required for data collection and analysis" (p. 8). For this study, purchase preference does not include buying directly from a charity engaged in a fund-raising event or activity where there was no involvement or relationship with a CRM sponsor. Respondents were only specifically asked to report their preference for purchasing a cause-related marketing (CRM) product from a CRM sponsor. These decisions were based on the time constraints of this study and the nature of demographic questions to measure affiliation, which do not require further discussion or information from the respondent.

Significance of the Study

The significance of the problem lay not so much with the organizations engaged in CRM as with the significant need of charities for funding. Bellett (2010) claimed, "The stock market crash of 2008 and the bailout of banks and multi-national corporations shook the economic foundations of governments, and with money evaporating overnight, it was no surprise charities were among the first to feel the pinch" (p. 4). Charities received funding from wealthy individuals, foundations, corporations, and governments. The Great Recession of 2008 impacted funds from all sources. Al-Tabbaa, Gadd, and Ankrah (2013) stated, "Issues such as uncertainty of government funding and the decline of private donations due to economic difficulties, coupled with growing competition within and outside the sector, render the survival of non-profit organizations to a more difficult task" (p. 590). This would have included seeking increasingly creative ways to help people and organizations participate in CRM campaigns.

During the Great Recession of 2008, as donations dwindled and grants went away, charities were forced to fiercely compete for remaining grants against many more applicants than before. More time and effort was put into searching for and attracting individual donors; with the financial well-being of donors devastated by the stock market crash, donors became more conservative. Andreasen and Kotler (2009) explained, "In the dot-com boom years in 2000 and 2001, several central collection sites sprang up, but many quickly disappeared when the boom deflated and when donors did not rush to the sites" (p. 395). The limited availability of and greater competition for financial grants coupled with a reduction in contributions to charities has placed a greater dependence on for-profit organizations with a CRM mission. "Previously funded through government structures, many charities are turning to the for-profit sector for financial support and are increasingly employing marketing practices" (Runte, Basil, & Deshpande, 2009, p. 255). Luckily, for-profit organizations came to the rescue with a new strategy for increasing donations to the charities: CRM. Over the years, CRM has proven its value to CRM sponsors and supported the existence and growth of charities desperate for funding in the most recent of economic downturns (2008-2016). Consequently, improving the marketing and sales of CRM campaign products was greatly needed to continue the good work provided by charities.

Understanding the behavior of consumers who had a strong level of affiliation to charities could make a significant impact on target marketing and market segmentation for CRM campaigns. Determining the most effective ways to identify lucrative target markets for CRM campaigns presented a better understanding of the relationship between affiliation and purchase preference. This required a keen perception of the information the consumer brought to the purchase setting. Grau and Folse (2007) stated, "We believe that consumer traits could prove to be important aspects of CRM campaign development that require greater attention from researchers" (p. 30). Marketing managers customarily used purchase behavior in their strategic marketing decisions; yet, the relationship between affiliation and purchase preference has yet to be clearly defined.

Definitions of Terms

To create a common frame of reference, the vocabulary and acronyms used in this research have been defined.

Affiliation: "An individual's relationship to a charity. The consumer and the consumer's immediate family members and close friends who currently or in the past were an employee of, a volunteer with, a beneficiary of, or a donor (product or money) to a charity" (Kuntz-Azan, 2016).

Beneficiary: "Someone who has received something of value from a charity such as a scholarship, help with housing or utilities, hospice care, or room and board at a Ronald McDonald House" (Kuntz-Azan, 2016).

Cause-Related Marketing (CRM): "A marketing program that attempts to achieve two goals – improving corporate performance and helping worthy causes by connecting fund raising for the benefit of a cause to the purchase of a firm's products" (Varadarajan & Menon, 1988, p. 58).

Cause-Related Marketing Campaign: "A marketing campaign which blends a CRM sponsor's product with a charitable cause in which "a corporation contributes a share of the proceeds for each unit of its product sold to the designated social cause" (Eikenberry, 2013, p. 290).

Cause-Related Marketing Product: "Something offered by a CRM sponsor to benefit a charity in either proceeds or in-kind products" (Kuntz-Azan, 2016).

Charity Affiliation: "An individual's relationship to a charity. The consumer and the consumer's immediate family members and close friends who currently or in the past were an employee of, a volunteer with, or a donor (product or money) to a charity" (Kuntz-Azan, 2016).

Charity: "A group organized for purposes other than generating profit and in which no part of the organization's income is distributed to its members, directors, or officers. The sole purpose is to benefit the public" (Forester, 2013).

Consumer: "One who purchases a product or service" (Kuntz-Azan, 2016).

Corporate Social Responsibility (CSR): "Activities sponsored by an organization that are not regulated or required by the government, including both internal and external CSR" (Carboy-Hall, 2005).

Cause-Related Marketing Donation Practices: "CRM donation practices identify the amount of the CRM sponsor's donation to the charity from the sale of a CRM campaign product. There are five basic "CRM donation practices" advertised in CRM campaigns. (1) a percentage of the price you pay for the CRM campaign product, (2) a percentage of the proceeds from your purchase of the CRM campaign product, (3) a set dollar amount of the purchase price that you pay for the CRM campaign product, (4) a product similar to the product you purchase, and (5) CRM donation practice is not specified in the CRM campaign and it simply states a donation will be made when you make a purchase" (Kuntz-Azan, 2016).

Cause-Related Marketing Sponsor: "A for-profit organization that sponsors a cause-related marketing campaign" (Kuntz-Azan, 2016).

Donor: "Someone who has given money, food, clothing or household items to a charity" (Kuntz-Azan, 2016).

Employee: "An employee is one who is working at a for-profit and/or a charity for wages" (Kuntz-Azan, 2016).

Feelings: "Intentional responses to values" (King, 2001, p. 51).

Immediate Family: "The respondent's spouse, children, parents, and siblings" (Kuntz-Azan, 2016).

Manufacturer: "Maker of the CRM campaign product" (Kuntz-Azan, 2016).

Market Segmentation: "The process of aggregating individuals or businesses along similar characteristics that pertain to the use, consumption, or benefits of a product or service" (Strauss & Frost, 2014, p. 199).

Motivation: "The hypothetical construct used to describe the internal and/or external forces that produce the initiation, direction, intensity and persistence of behavior" (Vallerand, 2012, p. 45).

Partner: "One with whom you are in a committed relationship, but not married to" (Kuntz-Azan, 2016).

Perception: "A way of regarding, understanding, or interpreting external stimuli" (Oxford University Press, 2008).

Purchase Preference: "The choices made by consumers as to which products to consume" (Pass, Davies, & Lowes, 2006, p. 316).

Successful Cause-Related Marketing Campaigns:
"Meeting or exceeding goals and/or targeted
outcomes for CRM campaigns" (Kuntz-Azan,
2016).

Tampa Bay Area: "Tampa, St. Petersburg and
Clearwater, Florida Metropolitan Statistical Area"
(http://www.census.gov).

Target Marketing: "The process of selecting the
market segments that are most attractive to the
company" (Strauss & Frost, 2014, p. 199).

Targeting Strategy: "The process of selecting a
segment of the population as the focal point of
marketing communication" (Wang, 2014, p. 42).

Transaction: "An exchange of something of value
between each party" (Kotler, 1972).

Unsuccessful Cause-Related Marketing Campaigns:
"Not meeting or exceeding goals and/or targeted
outcomes for CRM campaigns" (Kuntz-Azan,
2016).

Values: "Beliefs or guiding principles regarding what is truly important; the ideals that give significance to our lives" (Johnston, 2002, p. 7).

Volunteer: "Someone who gives their time to a charity" (Kuntz-Azan, 2016).

Willingness to Pay: "The maximum price a buyer is willing to pay" (Barber, Pei, Bishop, & Goodman, p. 286).

CHAPTER TWO:

REVIEW OF THE LITERATURE

Introduction

This literature review supporting the research was divided into five themes: (a) corporate social responsibility, (b) cause-related marketing (CRM), (c) CRM marketing strategy and segmentation, (d) affiliation, and (e) purchase preference. These themes were supported by synthesized information from existing marketing literature. The purpose of the literature review was not to duplicate knowledge already developed, but to provide a comprehensive investigation of relevant scholarly findings extracted from primary and secondary source material (Creswell, 2005).

Understanding how affiliation with a charity impacts the consumer's purchase preference for CRM campaign products significantly impacted the success of a CRM campaign and its partners. Determining the nature and strength of consumer affiliations assisted with segmenting the market and selecting the most appropriate segments of consumers to target for a CRM campaign. Over the years, much of the academic research had turned to the nuances of CRM and provided insights into the strategies and components related to such a strategy. Although other studies have investigated CRM from a variety of angles, this study explored consumer affiliations with charities and their purchase preference for products of CRM campaigns.

Corporate Social Responsibility

The highly publicized and documented breaches in ethics and gross negligence at corporations such as Enron, Arthur Anderson, and British Petroleum (BP) along with the former NASDAQ chairman and fallen giant, Bernard Madoff, led to devastating outcomes for company stakeholders. Consequently, the public had less confidence in for-profit organizations, and stakeholders had become increasingly skeptical of big business. Demetriou, Papasolomou, and Vrontis (2010) observed, "As the public's skepticism increases, firms have begun to realize that consumers expect greater corporate social responsibility" (p. 266).

Corporate Social Responsibility (CSR) encompassed the expectation that corporations engaged in pro-social behavior. According to Mohr et al. (2001), "There is a growing literature attempting to define what it means for a company to be socially responsible. A major question for business historically has been whether corporate decision makers should be concerned with issues other than profitability" (p. 46). Adam Smith (1863) argued that "business owners, in the pursuit of profit, will ultimately produce the greatest social good because of the invisible hand of the marketplace" (p. 46).

The public had become much more aware of socially responsible organizations, especially with the rise of the millennial generation; stakeholders were now demanding it. In response to the public's outcry for more social responsibility from corporations, "Some organizations embraced social responsibility as a part of their overall marketing efforts and as a means of improving consumer attitudes towards brand and the firm" (Thomas, 2007, p. 64). Corporations were taking their CSR strategy more serious, given the growing sentiments of consumers with respect to this practice. Organizations were also focusing on maintaining long-term relationships with their stakeholders. Responsive organizations were increasingly looking for additional ways to improve their reputations.

Another outgrowth of this highly public dilemma was creation of the Corporate Social Responsibility Index Study (2010) that discussed how companies' reputations were affected by public perceptions of performance related to citizenship, governance, and workplace practices. These 2010 results showed companies were improving socially responsible practices and the public was increasingly more aware and interested in these efforts" (bcccc.net/pdf/CSRIReport2010.pdf). The more public attention on these studies and the clustering of corporate stocks based on the company's level of social responsibility or their index ranking, the more pressure these organizations would be to conform to new social responsibility standards and expectations.

Corporate social responsibility had become ever present, taking many forms, one of which is CRM. Thomas (2007) clarified, "CRM refers to CSR activities that include offers to consumers to contribute a portion of the price of the product or service to a charitable organization" (p. 14). Vanhamme et al. (2012) asserted, "Despite increasing trends of cause-related marketing and corporate social responsibility in general, the idea of being socially responsible, beyond the formal scope of business activities, still is relatively new" (p. 264).

Liston-Heyes and Liu (2013) discussed how "firms increasingly rely on cause-related marketing (CRM) to manage public expectations of their corporate social responsibilities (CSR)" (p. 5). They further suggested, "CRM is instrumental in developing positive attitudes toward a corporate brand" (Liston-Heyes & Liu, 2013, p. 5). Consumers have favorable attitudes toward companies that supported a cause, but some were suspicious of the CRM sponsor's motives. Their suspicion surrounded the increase in profits CRM sponsors received from the CRM campaigns relative to the amount of donations that charities received from these campaigns. Although there was no hard-and-fast rule for the amount of contribution to the amount of profits ratio, consumers continued to wonder how this partnership was working and – was their purchase of a CRM campaign product helping the charity enough? – in their eyes.

Not surprising, some "consumers wish to reward companies for conscientious behaviors" (Folse, Niedrich, & Gru, 2010, p. 306). Consumer rewards included purchasing stock and products from socially responsible corporations or purchasing products offered by their-partner CRM campaigns. According to a Cone (2006) study of young consumers, "79% indicated they are likely to purchase that company's products, 44% are likely to actively pursue working at that company, and 74% are more likely to pay attention to the message of the company because it has a deep commitment to a cause" (as cited in Furlow, 2011, p. 62).

Cause-Related Marketing (CRM)

In 1984, American Express was extremely innovative starting a trend by "creating a link between product usage or purchase and charitable donations. American Express pledged a penny to the restoration project for the Statue of Liberty for each transaction made by a card member and a dollar for any new credit card opened. Rozensher (2013) wrote, "Over a million dollars was ... raised and cardholder transaction activity was boosted by an astounding 29%" (p. 181). Furthermore, "American Express was able to copyright the term they used to describe it as cause-related marketing" (Rifon & Trimble, 2002, p. 273). Since then cause-related marketing, "also known as cause marketing, cause-brand partnerships, or cause tie ins has been the subject of continuing debate and change, while growing in importance and prevalence" (Rozensher, 2013, p. 181).

The concept of CRM was introduced to the academic world by Varadarajan and Menon in the late 1980s. At that time, Varadarajan and Menon (1988) defined CRM as, "a marketing program that attempts to achieve two goals – improving corporate performance and helping worthy causes by connecting fund raising for the benefit of a cause to the purchase of a firm's products" (p. 58). Serban,

Iconaru, and Perju (2012) added, "The purpose of cause-related marketing is to attract consumers that want to make a difference in society by their purchasing. It is maintained that when faced with products of similar quality and prices, consumers will prefer the ones that are linked to a social cause" (p. 27).

Campaigns

A CRM campaign linked a sponsor and the sponsor's product with a charity in which its sponsor "contributes a share of the proceeds for each unit of its product sold to the designated social cause" (Eikenberry, 2013, p. 290). Since the inception in 1984 of the American Express campaign for the Statue of Liberty's renovations, a "multitude of companies have aligned themselves with worthy causes, creating mutually beneficial relationships" (Grau & Folse, 2007, p. 20). "Over the decade of the 1990s, corporate spending on cause-related marketing campaigns increased over 500 percent" (Rifon & Trimble, 2002, p. 273). "In 2006, 1.3 billion were spent on CRM campaigns in the United States"

(Runte, Basil, & Deshpande, 2009, p. 255).

As the success of CRM campaigns grew, so did the number of sponsors and charities engaged in and considering a cause-related marketing strategy. Folse, Niedrich, and Grau (2010) informed, "As recently as 2009, 100% of Fortune 500 manufacturers and retailers indicated that CRM was a committed portion of their strategic plan and that they will remain committed to their involvement in CRM" (p. 295). Consequently, the use of promised donations to a charity as a purchase incentive had become common in today's marketplace.

As CRM campaigns grew, their strategies have changed significantly over the years (Rifon & Trimble, 2002). Although CRM began with "companies donating to a charity each time a consumer purchases a specific product," many models of CRM have emerged (Anuar, Omar, & Mohamad, 2013, p. 195). Eikenberry (2013) wrote, "There are a range of CRM models, the best known of which is the transactional model, in which a corporation contributes to a designated social cause a share of the proceeds for each unit of its products sold" (p. 291). Two examples of the transactional model are the Susan B. Komen pink products campaign and the Product Red campaign. Both campaigns ran in partnership with multinational corporations in the US and elsewhere, and through these campaigns the consumer who purchased a CRM campaign product also supported breast cancer research (Komen) or the HIV/AIDS fight in Africa (RED) (Eikenberry, 2013).

Two other CRM campaign models are the promotion-based model and licensing-based model:

The promotion based model involves a corporation promoting a cause and making a contribution to a charity that is not necessarily tied to a transaction and not necessarily monetary. An example is the partnership between the Anti-Defamation League and Barnes & Noble. The "Close the Book on Hate" initiative provides instructional materials and lectures to promote racial and cultural tolerance. (Eikenberry, 2013, p. 291)

The licensing-based model allowed the CRM sponsor to license the charity's name and logo for use on the sponsor's CRM campaign product and in their advertising in exchange for a percentage of every purchase or an in-kind product (Eikenberry, 2013). One example was the relationship between the World Wildlife Fund and Visa.

The following were examples of CRM partnerships and campaigns: Yoplait Yogurt and New Balance with the Susan G. Komen Foundation; Kay Jewelers with St. Jude Research Children's Hospital; Wendy's and Dave Thomas' Foundation for Adoption; Starbucks and the Oprah Winfrey Leadership Academy Foundation; Barnes & Noble and the Anti-Defamation League; Nabisco and the World Wildlife Fund; Visa and the World Wildlife Fund; Cumberland Farms and the ALS Association; Unilever partnered with Direct Relief; and Hershey's campaign with UNICEF.

The complexity of academic CRM research and CRM campaigns lay in the various components of a CRM campaign that included: the CRM sponsor's brand, the charity's brand, the product and the CRM donation practice. Consumer behavior was always complex and particularly unique to CRM campaigns. CRM campaigns can be a highly effective strategy for improving consumer's perceptions of the CRM sponsor. Successful CRM campaigns were built by selecting the right combination of sponsor, charity, product, and CRM donation practice.

Partnerships

Successful CRM campaigns were built with the right combination of sponsor, charity, product, and CRM donation practice. Demetriou, Papasolomou, and Vrontis (2010) explained,

> *To form a successful partnership, great mutual effort and dedication is needed. Results have to be long-term-rather than short-term oriented, and the expectations of the two partners have to be clearly defined in advance so as to avoid conflict, stress and dissatisfaction, which may ruin the reputation of both organizations" (p. 271).*

Liu and Ko's (2011) study showed, "the potential alliance partner (for either side), who confirms all the legitimacy expectations (i.e. market legitimacy) of the focal organization, is also more likely to meet the focal organization's objective of collective strength" (p. 258).

Unfortunately, sponsor organizations often selected their CRM partner for reasons other than improving the bottom line of their organization or attracting the highest number of consumers possible to support the charity through consumer purchases. Top leaders often adopted a cause personally close to them. Sometimes it was a cause for an illness they or their family had experienced or a cause to support their children. Some sponsors delegated the choice of a charity to a committee for recommendations. Although noble, the adoption of a charity was an important decision for the successful implementation of a CRM strategy. In the end, certain types of charities worked best with certain types of sponsors and products.

A selection of a charity's CRM sponsor could be an important decision. Not just any charity works with any for-profit sponsor and its CRM campaign product. Some CRM campaigns did not succeed when mismatched partnerships and products failed to gain consumer support. The cause needed to provide both a national and local connection to drive sales.

Thomas (2005) stated, "If there is no opportunity to move a product, the marketer won't be motivated to make a financial commitment to the cause" (p. 71).

Another mismatch area could have been the value of the sponsor and charity's branding, as well as the product's brand. Each partner's brand contributed to the success of a CRM campaign. Sometimes the value of each partner's brand was not equal, allowing for the partner with the less valuable brand to increase their brand value by association. The distance between the values of the partners' brand was an issue in selecting the right partner to ensure success, just as the product's brand. For example, a CRM campaign between a dessert shop and charity supporting diabetic education was a mismatch for both entities. Logically and visually these two entities had different missions, strategies, and supporters. Another example of a mismatch of sponsor, charity, and product could be seen in the partnership between Susan G. Komen Breast Cancer Foundation and Kentucky Fried Chicken, in which part of the sales from a bucket of chicken goes to the foundation. Eikenberry's (2013) research explained how Waters, a blogger and supporter of CRM wrote:

"With 2400 calories and 160 grams of fat, a bucket of extra crispy KFC should include the wig you will need for cancer treatments after eating this crap for years" (p. 293).

At times throughout a CRM campaign, both partners need to reevaluate the value their CRM partner brought to their mission and the success of the CRM campaign. Changing partners was a serious decision with far-reaching consequences within the organization and throughout the marketplace. Such a change would not be a quiet one, attracting much attention with questions of why and what happened, not to mention the associated rumors.

When a CRM campaign did not gain momentum, either partner may consider if the product was the right one, if their partner was the right one, and/or if their target market was the right one. There were some concerns for 'less marketable' causes. Grau and Folse's (2007) research indicated, "Some causes are "less marketable" (e.g., prostate cancer), are not high-profile causes, or are chronic problems (hunger and homelessness) that have problems sustaining high-involvement levels" (p. 20).

A new charity also meant a new strategy and organization identity in the marketplace that required both marketing and public relations professionals to be involved. A successful new launch enhanced the sponsor's reputation affiliated with the new beneficiary of their CRM mission. Such far-reaching changes may have greatly improve inter-partner synergy leading to a greater competitive advantage in the market place and the sponsor's strategic group. In addition to the organizational changes from changing partners, there may have been turmoil with leaders who had personal affiliations with the current charity. Problems may not only arise from the fusion of incompatible philosophies, but also from practicality and relevance. (Robson, & Dunk, 1999, p. 229). These leaders may have resisted needed changes for their organization's success, which may have resulted in new leadership.

Grau and Folse (2007) confirmed, "A multitude of companies have aligned themselves with worthy causes, creating mutually beneficial relationships" (p. 20). There was added value when the CRM sponsors had specifically linked themselves to charities related to the CRM sponsor's product. For example, "Purina

Pet Foods has had promotional campaigns involving saving endangered animals, supporting the local zoo, and sponsoring a program that provides pets for senior citizens and the disabled" (Strahilevitz & Myers, 1998, p. 445).

Austin (2003) proposed a collaboration continuum, which included three stages of collaboration between CRM sponsors and charities. The first stage was the Philanthropic Stage. This was the period when a charity approached a sponsor for a donation. If the sponsor felt it wanted to contribute, and had the resources, a donation was made. The second stage was the Transactional Stage - when the sponsor and charity discussed partnering for events and campaigns (traditional CRM activities). The third stage was the Integrative Stage. This was when long-term relationships and strategic alliances form between the sponsor and the charity. Organizational missions and brands would have sometimes aligned.

Often, organizations select their CRM partner for reasons other than improving the financial bottom line or for attracting the highest number of consumers possible. "A marketer who wants to adopt a CRM program must be aware of the fact that well-implemented and well-promoted CRM programs have the potential to bring enormous benefits to the partnership" (Demetriou, Papasolomou, & Vrontis, 2010, p. 267).

Consequently, the organizations engaged in CRM with the charity benefit from co-marketing, enhanced company individual brands, provided greater name recognition, and strengthened the affiliation with each other in the eyes of consumers.

Cause-Related Marketing Sponsors

There had been an upsurge in CRM with CRM sponsors and the strategy continues to gain attention. Grau and Folse (2007) posited, "Company reports and research offer numerous CRM success stories and reports that promote the potential gains for both the for-profit and non-profit partners" (p. 19). "The company that has chosen the conventional delivery pattern aims directly to deliver the social benefits to the cause and marketing messages to the relevant audiences through adopting a particular CRM implementation strategy" (Liu & Ko, 2011, p. 253). Runte, Basil, and Deshpande agreed, "Cause-related marketing as a strategic marketing tool to increase profitability has been an assumed goal of corporate engagement, but corporations may also use CRM to communicate core values to society" (p. 257).

Cause-related marketing sponsors "benefit because the campaigns are profit motivated. That is, donations are made based on consumer behavior, which is most often exercised by purchasing the sponsoring company's product" (Grau & Folse, 2007, p. 20). Cause-related marketing sponsors benefited from an increase in their sales of CRM campaign products contributing to their bottom line. Eikenberry (2013) suggested that CRM sponsors, "potentially increase sales and publicity for their products, improve their image, expand target markets, increase consumer identifications with the company, and provide employees and customers with a sign that they 'care' about the community" (p. 292).

Even with an upsurge in CRM campaigns, several for-profit organizations remained hesitant to jump on the CRM bandwagon. These for-profit organizations may have been uncertain how to proceed with such a strategy, how to identify their market, how to best reach a CRM market, and lastly, how profitable such an endeavor would be for them.

Consequently, these for-profit organizations were simply watching the impact on the CRM sponsors that have already adopted a CRM mission.

While hesitant organizations hold back, CRM campaigns continued to flourish providing a variety of models for these wavering organizations considering a CRM campaign. Enhanced strategic marketing could be financially advantageous for the CRM organizations and personally beneficial to their consumers. As charity managers become more selective and/or demanding of CRM sponsors seeking CRM relationships, CRM sponsors may be more aggressive giving closer attention to marketing CRM campaign products.

Charitable Non-Profit Organizations (Charities)

Runte et al. (2009) stated, "Non-profit organizations engage in corporate sponsorships for multiple reasons, some of which are oriented to satisfy the operational needs of the non-profit organization, such as attaining funding to support program operation. Additionally, they engage in partnerships to further their mission in terms of cause recognition" (p. 260). "Concurrent with the escalation in CSR expectations placed upon the profit sector, the non-profit sector has faced increased pressures for accountability and financial efficiency" (Runte et al., 2009, p. 255). There were a number of charities in competition for funding. The limited availability of and greater competition for financial grants coupled with a reduction in contributions to charities had placed greater dependence on CRM sponsors with a CRM mission. "Previously funded through government structures, many charities are turning to the for-profit sector for financial support and are increasingly employing marketing practices" (Runte et al., 2009, p. 255).

Taylor (2012) observed, "Since 1995, when this data was first tracked, the number of non-profit organizations registered with the Internal Revenue Service (IRS) has increased 68% percent, numbering over 1.5 million in 2011" (p. 12). The increase in non-profit organizations included charitable organizations as well as non-profit organizations that were not charities. The increase in charitable organizations created a greater need for funding, which at first resulted in central collection sites for groups of charities. In the dot-com boom years of 2000 and 2001, many of these central collection sites "quickly disappeared when the boom deflated" and "donors did not rush to the sites" (Andreasen & Kotler, 2008, p. 395). Then "the stock market crash of 2008 and the bailout of banks and multinational corporations shook the economic foundations of governments, and with so much money evaporating overnight, it was no surprise that charities and non-profits were among the first to feel the pinch" (Bellett, 2010, p. 4).

> *Consequently, charitable organizations in the United States have increasingly adopted market-based revenue-generating approaches to sustain operations and meet service demands. The reasons are many and they include an increased need for non-profit and voluntary organizations (and for-profits) to "replace" government in the provision of public goods and services in the face of the cutbacks, privatization, and relatively limited or tepid growth of charitable giving over the past several decades. (Eikenberry, 2013, p. 290)*

Al-Tabbaa, Gadd, and Ankrah (2013) stated, "Issues such as uncertainty of government funding and the decline of private donations due to economic difficulties, coupled with the growing competition within and outside the sector, render the survival of NPOs to a more difficult task" (p. 590). Although charities received funding from sources such as wealthy individuals, foundations, corporations, and governments, the Great Recession impacted funds from all sources. Oberg (2011) stated, "the Great Recession began in December of 2007, and was approximately 18 months in duration, and was followed by a weak and jobless recovery that has persisted into the second decade of this century" (p. 553). During the Great Recession, as donations dwindled and grants went away, charities were forced to fiercely compete for the remaining grants against many more applicants than ever before. More time and effort was put into searching for and attracting individual donors; however, with the financial well-being of donors devastated by the stock market crash, donors became more conservative. The limited availability of and greater competition for grants coupled with a reduction in contributions to charities had placed greater dependence on for-profit organizations with a CRM mission. Consequently, many charities "are turning to the for-profit sector for financial support and are increasingly employing marketing practices" (Runte, Basil & Deshpande, 2009, p. 255).

Eikenberry (2013) concluded, "One market-based revenue-generating approach that charitable organizations are increasingly relying upon in the United States and around the world is fundraising through cause-related marketing (p. 290). Eikenberry's (2013) study further discussed how organizers of campaigns choose CRM to raise money. "This seems to be the main motivation for many charities. Organizers see CRM as an avenue for raising much-needed funds in a tough economy and an environment where government funding and donations have been cut or have remained stagnant in the past several years" (Eikenberry, 2013, p. 300).

Consequently, charities enjoy several benefits and value the relationships they had with CRM sponsors. "CRM campaigns improve a charity's ability to continue with their mission by increasing resources and awareness" (Grau & Folse, 2007, p.

20). Eikenberry (2013) added, "Charities appear to gain legitimacy in the marketplace that they might not have previously possessed, generate financial resources, gain additional volunteers, increase public confidence, and elevate the image of the cause or charity" (p. 292). Charities looked to CRM sponsors to form relationships for CRM campaigns, not only as a means for funding, but for public relations as well.

Runte et al. (2009) found, "Non-profit organizations appear to be primarily seeking event support as well as opportunities for networking and increasing public awareness when they enter into CRM alliances" (p. 265). Runte et al. (2009) further stated, "Partnerships between corporations with strong reputations and non-profit organizations with little prior public awareness stimulate an increase in trust, awareness, and support for the non-profit organization" (p. 257). These relationships provided mutual benefits.

Charitable organizations also benefited from greater proceeds for their entire organization, as proceeds are often given to the parent organization, rather than a local branch. For example, Dress for Success operates a domestic and international non-profit organization with branches in various regions of the world. Proceeds to the parent Dress for Success organization filtered down to those branches, thus enhanced the reputation of the parent organization, as well as their local branches. The Dress for Success charitable, non-profit, organization also enjoyed greater publicity worldwide, which better informed and attracted potential employees, volunteers, and consumers, as well as donors of case and/or in-kind products (clothing and accessories) for all the branches. Hence, "While non-profits are facing limited resources to meet significant increases in demand, they are also looking at new fundraising strategies and opportunities for more meaningful relationships with supporters" (Taylor, 2012, p 13).

Sponsor's Cause-Related Marketing Campaign Product

Not only must sponsors and charities select the best partner for their CRM campaign, they must select the best product to attract consumers to make a CRM purchase. Product selection involved consideration of the type of product, its brand, the brand's loyalty among consumers, and its packaging.

The product itself was a major consideration for the sponsor engaging in a CRM campaign. Strahilevitz and Myers' (1998) cited three studies providing, "strong evidence that charity incentives are more effective with the feelings generated from frivolous products than with the more functional motivations associated with practical products" (p. 443). Frivolous products included Nabisco® animal cookies, Cottonelle® toilet paper, and Hershey's® chocolate (Strahilevitz & Myers, 1998). A key tag for Wendy's® Frosty ice cream shakes could also be considered a frivolous product.

Although Strahilevitz and Meyers (1998) suggested practical products were less successful in CRM campaigns, many successful campaigns had adopted a practical product. For instance, practical CRM campaign products have included Vaseline® lotion, petroleum jelly, and durable tote bags. As expected, more practical products often come with a higher price tag for consumers; some also carried special features or labeling to be considered more lasting and attractive to consumers. Frivolous or practical, a CRM campaign product included its packaging. CRM packaging often displayed advertising for the CRM campaign as a notification and reminder of the campaign and its attributes to the consumer.

A product's brand impacts a consumer's perception of the product's quality and value. Brand loyalty was highly valued, enhancing the success of a CRM campaign. Some common shopping and spending traits had been shown to impact loyalty to a specific product brand or to a specific manufacturer. This has been found to be true in older clients (Baby Boomers and seniors) who were more likely not to purchase a substitute brand if their preferred brand was not available (Foxall, 1978). Frequent shoppers had lower brand loyalty and shoppers who socialized with neighbors showed higher brand loyalty (Foxall, 1978). Consequently, the brand loyalty of CRM consumers was a factor to be weighed by both parties before selecting a product for a CRM campaign.

Although most, if not all, packaging included CRM advertising, not all CRM campaign products carried a permanent label or feature identifying the CRM charity or campaign. Permanent identification with the CRM campaign was long lasting, thus sending a message of the consumer's support for the charity, that creates a visual constituency of followers, and further advertised the campaign. Consequently, the consumer's personal image was impacted by their association with their support of the charity involved in the CRM campaign when the product carried a permanent reminder of the CRM campaign. Finally, Elfenbein, and McManus (2010) explained, "It is noteworthy for those who study charitable fundraising strategies that demand for charity-linked products is higher than that for non-charity-linked products" (p. 55).

Cause-Related Marketing Donation Practices

Successful CRM campaigns were built by selecting the right combination of product, sponsor, charity, and CRM donation practice. CRM campaigns were contractual agreements between the sponsor and the charity, identifying the product and the CRM donation practice. Both parties were aware of the amount of donation from each purchase given to the charity. However, for the consumer, the clarity of the donation amount from the consumers' purchase was often lacking.

Cause-related marketing donation practices identified the amount of the CRM sponsor's donation to the charity from the sale of a CRM campaign product. There were five basic "CRM donation practices" advertised in CRM campaigns: "(1) a percentage of the price you paid for the CRM campaign product, (2) a percentage of the proceeds from your purchase of the CRM campaign product, (3) a set dollar amount of the purchase price that you paid for the CRM campaign product, (4) a product similar to the product you purchase, and (5) CRM donation practice was not specified in the CRM campaign, and it stated a donation would be made when you made a purchase" (Kuntz-Azan, 2016).

Some of these CRM donation practices seemed very clear on the amount to be donated to the charity; however, some were not as clear, leaving the consumer to wonder how much or what they are contributing to the charity with their purchase. Three of these CRM donation practices were unclear with respect to the language of the advertised CRM donation practice. How many consumers understood the meaning of 'proceeds?' Did consumers believe that proceeds were the same as profits; net or gross; sales, net or gross; or price? The meaning of proceeds was important to consumer understanding on how to calculate the amount they were donating via their CRM purchase to the charity to determine if the donation was worth the price and their support. As for 'in-kind' donations, consumers may or may not have understood the in-kind donation may not be exactly like the CRM campaign product they purchased. If the CRM campaign product was shoes and the consumer paid $40 for their shoes, did the sponsor's in-kind donation become an exact pair (style and size); any $40 shoe in inventory; any shoe at any price in inventory; or any shoe the recipient (charity) needs?

BOGO is 'buy-one-get-one free' or 'buy-one-give-one' suggesting the same item purchased is the same item given. Consumers may have assumed BOGO was 'same in-kind' when making a CRM purchase, only to find out the product given to charity was a different product and/or different in price or value. Simply advertising a donation will be made with a CRM purchase leaves the amount of donation up to the imagination of the consumer.

The lack of clarity in the advertised CRM donation practice begs the question of consumer trust in the sponsor to have donated the right amount to the charity, whatever that right amount may be. Consumers expected the sponsor to fulfill donation obligations to the charity. Consumers weighed the sponsor, the charity, the product, and the CRM donation practice with the typical purchase factors such as brand, price, warranty, quality, availability, and time sensitive pricing. When the consumers' purchase decision comes down to the feature of the product being attached to a cause, the consumer may decide not to make the purchase because something about the sponsor was unfavorable, untrustworthy, or questionable. Consequently, a CRM donation practice impacted the consumer's decision, if viewed as unclear or to be purposefully hiding the amount to be donated, thus making the sponsor appear to have been untrustworthy. This non-transparencly left the consumer uncertain about the amount of the actual donation and if the donation would actually be given to the charity.

The CRM donation practice was an economic factor, in part, representing the price of the CRM campaign product. When a sponsor selected a CRM campaign product for their campaign, the price or the product features may have been changed to attract consumers. Product features implied quality and there has been a long-standing assumption the relationship between price and quality was important for consumers. The consumer's evaluation of CRM donation practice, price, and quality was an undeniable relationship for consideration by consumers and sponsors. Furthermore, the consumer's perception of the various CRM donation practices was an important factor in the sponsor's decision to price the CRM campaign product.

Ethical Dilemmas

Cause-related marketing has a strong relationship to corporate image, "The public will respect organizations that acknowledge that a program helps their bottom line while benefiting a major social cause" (Andreasen & Kotler, 2008, p, 450). Nevertheless, there were potential risks involved, which included partner organization corruption, deception, and scandal. When considering CRM as a marketing strategy, both the charity and the CRM sponsor need to contemplate and mitigate these risks.

Cause-related marketing linked elements of corporate philanthropy with strategic marketing, thus there would be the threat of the future reputation of the chosen partner. The American Red Cross (ARC) was an example of a charity partner that faced a number of challenges due to handling factors during 9/11 in 2001 and Hurricane Katrina in 2005. The management at the ARC was widely criticized as being unethical. Ferrell, Fraedrich, and Ferrell (2011) explained, "The ARC had to address allegations of fraud, bribery, and even theft on the part of volunteers and employees. They have also faced a number of internal challenges due to high turnover, as well as charges of overcompensation and possible corruption among its board of directors and upper management" (p. 327).

The banking giant, HSBC provided an example of a CRM sponsor that suffered with a conflict in donation intent. "HSBC had donated $35 million to the Worldwide Fund for Nature to rescue threatened rivers, saved 20,000 rare plants, and trained more environmental scientists – a substantial sum and a good cause. But, it came under fire from the charity's staff because HSBC has also funded firms involved in the clearing of vast areas of virgin Indonesian rainforests and destruction of farms" (Mason, 2002, p. 11). The United Way scandal in 1992 revealed the president of the organization used donations to finance his personal lifestyle. This scandal impacted a variety of partners who were involved in CRM campaigns with The United Way at that time (Barnes, 1994). Once a partner organization was involved in any scandal that blemished its reputation, that blemish was also cast upon the partner organization(s).

According to Andreasen and Kotler (2008), organizations that developed a sound CRM strategy to mitigate potential risks included using board members, selecting a partner with a mutual interest, screening out partners who may present a conflict of interest, developing a carefully designed proposal, and making sure there was a clear role each partner would play. Andreasen and Kotler (2008) suggested using board members and community supporters to identify potential partners and to deflect possible future problems. Mutuality of interest had a number of advantages, including the public likely to being less suspicious of the for-profit organization's involvement. A non-profit should exclude partners whose product(s) conflicted with the non-profit's mandate, whose product was hazardous to health or the environment, that was under investigation for health, environment or other violations, and whose product and service claims, especially in the area of health, were unsubstantiated. Proposals should include how the organizations are well run and brands with no blemishes. The roles each partner would play, and what they will and will not do for each other can avoid awkward situations causing dysfunctional relationship conflicts, which could lead to public embarrassment, breach of contract lawsuits and a need to sever the partnership.

Taking into consideration the rise of corporate globalization, risks could also include negative press because of employees being culturally offended, which can cause mass boycotts of firms on an international level. This behavior results in decreased productivity, harming the international financial security of the firm (Silverthorne, 2009). Behavior could also harm the brand of the non-profit attached to the CRM sponsor. Consequently, potential ethical and moral dilemmas are a risk each partner takes while forming CRM partnerships and are a factor when considering CRM as a marketing strategy.

Globalization

Chang (2012) wrote, "Cause-related marketing (CRM) is becoming a world-wide trend" (p. 40). It is no wonder that CRM sponsors and charities have had an interest in globalization that presented a different set of considerations and risks. Wang (2014) explained, "With the global expansion of cause-related marketing (CRM), advertisers need to know whether and how cultural and societal differences impact attitude toward CRM across markets" (p. 41). Businesses needed to adjust their strategies to fit the surrounding environment and organizational characteristics to improve performance (Luo, 2005; Wang, 2014). Under this paradigm, CRM, as a type of business strategy, was conditioned by the surrounding market environment, including elements such as consumer traits (Luo, 2005; Wang, 2014).

Kumar (2000) explained, "researchers must acknowledge cultural mindset and that trends change in countries as the political leaders and international rules and regulations become less restrictive and more open to conducting global business" (p. 328). It was suggested organizations thoroughly understood cultural differences and orientations before entering any market. "Cultural orientations are defined as patterns of assumptions, beliefs, and perceptions (Hofstede, 1991) that drive people's attitude and behavior in a society" (Wang, 2014, p. 42). Examining other cultures' attitudes and behaviors in a society, prior to forming a globalization strategy, could avoid the unnecessary expense of wasting valued time and money, as well as embarrassment. "Many countries avoid doing business with the United States, Canada and France, because they have the reputation for developing strictly professional relationships, while India and Singapore seek trust and friendship first before they develop professional alliances" (Dorfman, 2004). Hofstede's research on cultural dimensions was often referred to while discussing cultural differences and/or cultural dimensions.

Wang (2014) explained, "This multi-dimensional view of individualism and collectivism redefines our understanding of culture and draws attention to the uncertainty of CRM in a cross-cultural setting. This uncertainty was partially due to interwoven relationships between collectivism, individualism, and consumers' attitude toward CRM" (p. 42). Previous studies had documented at least changes of cultural orientations across countries (Hofstede, 1991). For example, differences between individualism and collectivism may give rise to favorable or unfavorable perceptions of CRM (see Table 1).

Table 1: Individualism and Collectivism Domains Assessed in Individualism-Collectivism Scales

Individualism and Collectivism Domains Assessed in Individualism-Collectivism Scales		
Domain Name	*Description*	*Sample Item*
Individualism		
Independent	Freedom, self-sufficiency, and control of one's life	I tend to do my own thing and others in my family do the same.
Goals	Striving for one's own goals, desires, and achievements	I take great pride in accomplishing what no one else can accomplish.

Individualism and Collectivism Domains
Assessed in Individualism-Collectivism Scales

Domain Name	Description	Sample Item
Compete	Personal competition and winning	It is important to me that I perform better than others on a task.
Unique	Focus on one's unique, idiosyncratic qualities	I am unique – different from others in many respects.
Private	Thoughts and actions private from others	I like my privacy.
Self-Know	Knowing oneself; having a strong identity	I know my weaknesses and strengths
Direct Commun-ication	Clearly articulating one's wants and needs	I always state my opinions very clearly.
Collectivism		
Related	Considering close others an integral part of the self	To understand who I am, you must see me with members of my group.
Belong	Wanting to belong to and enjoy being part of groups	To me, pleasure is spending time with others.
Duty	The duties and sacrifices being a group member entails.	I would help, within my means, if a relative were in financial difficulty.
Harmony	Concern for group harmony and that groups get along	I make an effort to avoid disagreements with my group members.
Advice	Turning to close others for decision help	Before making a decision, I always consult with others.
Context	Self changes according to context or situation	How I behave depends on who I am with, where I am, or both.
Hierarchy	Focus on hierarchy and status issues	I have respect for the authority figures with whom I interact.
Group	I preference for group work.	I would rather do a group paper or lab than do one alone.

Resource:
http://psycnet.apa.org/journals/bul/128/1/images/bul_128_1_3_tbl1a.gif

Consequently, CRM in international markets requires firms to carefully analyze information to formulate appropriate strategies. It was important to examine key indicators such as political risk with expert ratings of stability, financial risk with rate of inflation and foreign exchange, and legal risk with import-export restrictions (Kumar, 2000). Marketing strategy, segmentation, and the selection of target customers was one of the basic strategies of an international marketer. Therefore, global "CRM strategies need to be adjusted to fit changes in consumer traits" (Wang, 2014, p. 49).

Cause-Related Marketing
Marketing Strategy and Segmentation

An efficacious marketing strategy was vital, and identifying an effective and unique approach was challenging. To achieve and sustain a competitive advantage, companies often adopted a differentiation strategy. Deac and Stanescu (2014) stressed "the need for a company to identify those ways through which it can truly differentiate, highlighting specialization in a specific activity" (p. 45). Taylor (2012) wrote a "competitive advantage is achieved through market segmentation targeting, and when studying relationship marketing; it is imperative to identify relationships that influence factors and use them to the benefit of the organization" (p. 4). For-profit sponsors and charities were engaging in CRM campaigns as part of their differentiation strategy. CRM differentiation benefited from highly defined market segmentation and targeting; however, defining characteristics of CRM consumers had yet to be done.

More defined market segments enhanced the efficiency and effectiveness of the sponsor's CRM marketing efforts. Sponsors began by identifying the most lucrative market segments for their CRM campaign product(s) and their partner charity. These market segments were then targeted with new segment-specific marketing plans to reach past consumers not affected by their past CRM marketing efforts while attracting new consumers unaware of the CRM campaign. Deac and Stanecu's (2014) study found:

In a practical approach to strategic segmentation one has to consider a number of strategic segmentation criteria or variables.

These criteria or strategic segmentation variables will allow, in most cases, making an initial strategic segmentation, indicating that they should be judged by the characteristics of a certain field of activity and based on these characteristics one may also consider other criteria (p. 461).

As market segmentation for CRM consumers became more defined, the sponsor's current CRM segmentation plans come under scrutiny, often times leading to new plans. When market segments changed, the old segments may be lost entirely, combined, or left as they were; however, new segments moved into positions of priority for evaluation and exploration of advertising and marketing strategies specific to the newer segmentation. Rather than dropping all current advertising, there may have been a slower transition to test the new segments with newer advertising. Newer segment-specific marketing plans and advertising impacted the sponsor's external contracts for CRM advertisements or if advertising and marketing efforts were in house operations, the activities of these groups changed quickly to the newer segmentation plans. Better aligned marketing and advertising improved the sponsor's competitiveness – both nationally and globally. If successful, new departments may have been created to better serve global markets and more employees from the international markets may have been hired. "Thus, just as they do within their domestic markets, international firms need to group their world markets into segments with distinct buying needs and behaviors" (Kotler & Armstrong, 2014, p. 201).

When CRM segments changed, the natural demographics of consumers within each CRM segment sometimes became very important. One such demographic was defined by the consumer's age and thus their generation, which cannot be ignored. Understanding each generation and what attracts those particular consumers was vital. No wonder marketers were embracing social media to attract consumers. Viewing all consumers in a segment as a single group was one approach to targeting and marketing to consumers for CRM campaign products. There were two important aspects of market segmentation: the basis of the segmentation and the impact of generational factors within the segment(s); both were important to the success of a CRM campaign. Generational factors centered on the largest generational segments in the marketplace: Baby Boomers and Millennials. Each of these generations were discussed relative to their size and the challenges of their generation for marketers of CRM campaigns. However, the basis of segmentation was the focus of this research study and was addressed in the section on 'Affiliation.'

Consumers in General

Consumers included volunteers at charities, employees of charities and sponsors, and stakeholders of sponsors and charities, and any other consumer evaluating products to purchase. Barber, Pei, Bishop and Goodman (2012) explained, "Attention has shifted to more in-depth studies of consumers so that manufacturers can effectively plan and evaluate their pricing, advertising, and promotional activities" (p. 280). Consumers were involved in purchasing CRM campaign products for a variety of reasons. Their reasons for supporting CRM campaigns varied from personal to simply obtaining a warm glowing feeling about their purchase involving a donation to a charity. Taylor (2012) stated, "Levy (1969) broadened the definition of marketing to include charitable activities, Kotler (1972) broadened the concept of transaction by defining it as an exchange of something of value between each party. In doing so, the criterion for exchange could be anything of value; for example, a donation or volunteer service in exchange for a warm, glowing feeling or gratification" (p. 19). As noted earlier, for many of these reasons, CRM campaigns were growing in support in the marketplace and board rooms.

Rozensher (2013) explained, "In 1993, an industry survey found that 66% of consumers supported the practice; in 2004, the Cone industry survey found 72% supported the practice. In 2010, American consumers showed no sign of tiring of these connections. An impressive 88% of consumers supported the practice and 83% said they wanted more of the products, services, and retailers that they use to partner with causes" (p. 181). Folse, Niedrich, and Grau (2010) found consumers expected firms to fulfill their donation obligation to the charity, as consumers evaluated a CRM campaign as an economic transaction. Eikenberry (2013) suggested, "Consumers may get additional information about a charity or cause and the chance to help the less fortunate or contribute to society in regular and convenient ways by using disposable rather than discretionary income" (p. 292).

Grau and Folse, 2007 posited, "Consumers find cause-driven partnerships a socially responsible means to contribute to the community. In addition, some consumers actually appear to enjoy the process of participating in campaigns" (p. 20). "Emotions can influence consumer attitudes; this is also true for consumer responses to CRM campaigns. One of the ample informational cues that humans integrate into their purchase decisions in this scope are assumptions about a firms' motivation to engage in CRM" (Moosemayer & Fuljahn, 2013, p. 205). Although many charities were thankful for sponsorship, their sponsors faced criticism from consumers that sponsors were thinking more about themselves than the charity to which they are aligned. Some consumers felt the sponsors' motives were focused on increasing the sponsor's profitability and market share, rather than for moral reasons. Consumers felt positive intentions prompted sponsors to engage in CRM, but some sponsors promoted skepticism among their consumers. "Such skepticism is beginning to surface in the marketplace where consumers are receiving warnings about the structure of campaigns" (Folse et al., 2010, p. 296). Sponsors could better manage the negative feelings about CRM by clarifying the sponsor's CRM donation practices in the CRM advertisements, publicizing how much money was donated to the charity, and how that money was used by the charity. Performing a better job at segmenting the CRM market, target marketing, improving profits, and giving more to the charity enhanced the sponsor's reputation with consumers and the charity.

Barbu (2013) contended, "As the market has changed to adopt new advertising techniques and consumer's input, market research faces times of great challenges – and great opportunities" (p. 430). Pei, Bishop, and Goodman (2012) suggested, "Attention has shifted to more in-depth studies of markets and consumers so that manufacturers can effectively plan and evaluate their pricing, advertising, and promotional activities" (p. 280). Grau and Folse (2007) maintained, "The majority of CRM campaigns implemented since their inception, offer consumers who are highly involved with causes a strong reason to participate" (p. 19). One such opportunity for research was to identify the less-involved consumers and determine the basis of their lack of involvement. This included uncovering how to engage consumers in CRM campaigns and purchase CRM campaign products. Grau and Folse (2007) suggested, "From a strategic viewpoint, gaining the attention of less-involved consumers has important implications for non-profit organizations. These less-involved consumers may be the key to future effectiveness for CRM campaigns as competition among companies allying with causes increases" (p. 19).

It was important for organizations to understand how to elicit the consumer behaviors that related to purchase preferences, including a thorough understanding of the consumer decision process (see Figure 2).

A. **Stages in the consumer decision-making process**

Problem recognition		Information search		Alternative evaluation		Purchase decision		Postpurchase evaluation

B. **Relevant internal psychological processes**

Motivation		Perception		Attitude formation		Integration		Learning

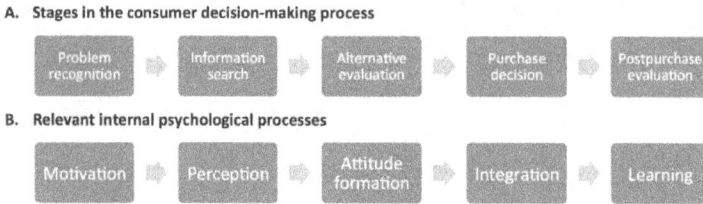

Figure 1 - Consumer Decision-Making Model

The consumer decision process directly intersected between the marketing strategy and the outcomes (Lamb, Hair, & McDaniel, 2013). Understanding consumer decision making, buying behavior, and confidence levels directly affected marketers and all those who involved in developing a CRM campaign. Organizations that adopted a CRM mission found it crucial to evaluate all aspects of consumers who were purchasing CRM campaign products to ensure the sponsor-charity relationship provided both parties with the most beneficial results.

Consumers, in general, were differentiated by their generation. Each generation learned different lessons and valued different things from the time in history in which they grew up. The larger the numbers in the generation, the more important they and their values were to the market segments into which they fell. Three of the largest generations at this point in history were the Baby Boomers, Millennials, and the rapidly emerging Generation Z.

Baby Boomers as Consumers

Baby Boomers were born between 1946 and 1964 and upon becoming adults, began their takeover of the consumer market one year at a time. Baby Boomers redefined their lives through partial or full retirement while making up 29% of the 2015 workforce (www.pewresearch.org). According to Gallup Daily tracking research in December 2015, self-reported daily spending among Americans aged 50-64 years old had rebounded to a 5-year high of $105 per day. These spending patterns mattered to marketers who hoped Baby Boomers would spend discretionary income with the marketing companies (http://www.gallup.com).

Haggerty (2013) asserted, "Just keep your eyes open as you go about your daily business and you will see an older population in the workforce" and in the marketplace (p. 2). "A major issue affecting Baby Boomers is their desire to remain in the work force, and stay engaged. Whereas previous generations longed to retire, many Baby Boomers fear becoming disengaged from friends and society" (Gibaldi, 2014, p. 51). Consequently, "the Baby Boomer generation is presently redefining retirement, and will continue to redefine retirement" (Gibaldi, 2014, p. 50).

Those Baby Boomers living on Social Security and pensions are, first, at a stage of life where their needs have changed and, second, limited in the amount of money they can earn while maintaining their Social Security and pensions. These two lifestyle changes were resulting in Baby Boomers with extra time, less purchasing power, and very different needs. In particular, the reduction in Baby Boomers' income created challenges for the marketers of products. No longer did Baby Boomers buy what they want; they buy what they need and with their needs changing, so must CRM campaign products and their marketing.

First, there was a need to supplement their retirement income (Haggerty, 2013). "Many seniors continue to work because of health-care and prescription expenses, minimal interest on savings accounts, and little latitude to trim everyday expenses" (Haggerty, 2013, p. 1). Those with part-time work had more disposable income and purchasing power in the marketplace for CRM campaign products. "Consumers may contribute to society in regular and convenient ways by using disposable rather than discretionary income" (Eikenberry, 2013, p. 292). However, price was an issue for the Baby Boomers and resulted in being an issue for the pricing of CRM campaign products.

Second, Baby Boomers felt a need to give back and they are doing so by volunteering time to charities. Nelson (2015) stated, "There are currently 76 million members of this generation living in the US; more than 20 million are volunteers" (www.nonprofitquarterly.com). When health issues prevented Baby Boomers from volunteering, CRM campaigns and products provided an alternative. Baby Boomers fulfilled a need to give back with their purchase of CRM campaign products they needed and could afford. This made the choice of CRM campaign products important when targeting Baby Boomers. Can Baby Boomers afford a CRM campaign product and do they need it in their lives?

Millennials as Consumers

Millennials, born between 1981 and 1997, were taking over the workplace and the marketplace in record numbers. "These children of the Baby Boomers number 83 million or more dwarfing the Gender's and becoming larger than the Baby Boomer segment" (Kotler & Keller, 2012, p. 78). Moreover, "They make up 34% of the 2015 workforce and 21% of the consumer market with an estimate of over a trillion dollars in purchasing power" (www.pewresearch.org). Millennials were making and demanding rapid changes to the consumer market. Millennials were loyal to brands they trusted and respected, but they were skeptical of advertising. Furlow (2011) stated, "Therein lies the beauty of cause marketing. These consumers are searching for an emotional connection to companies and brands, and what better way than for a company to gain the trust of Millennials, but to partner up with a popular social cause" (p. 62).

The Millennial generation grew up in tough economic times that sparked their interest in helping non-profit organizations and giving to those in need. Their association with charities was cemented with their high schools requiring community service and that service was an important factor in scholarships, grants, and admission to colleges and universities of their choice. "The National Society of High School Scholars recognizes top scholars who have demonstrated outstanding leadership, scholarship and community commitment" (Corcoran, 2015, p. 15). Coupled with an increased emphasis by colleges and universities to provide leadership experiences, Millennials continued their service to others – sometimes for college credit.

After graduation, Millennials began speaking with their dollars. Peterson (2009) posited, "Cone's 2006 survey indicated 70 percent of Millennials had purchased a product that supports a cause in the past year, and nearly 90 percent said they would switch from one company to another to support a cause" (p. 9). "The 2006 Cone Millennial Cause Study, found 74 percent of Millennials surveyed said they are likely or very likely to switch from one brand to another if the second brand is associated with a cause (price and quality being equal)" (Demetriou, Papasolomou, &

Vrontis, 2010, p. 271).

Now, "Millennials exhibit their own forms of participation, volunteering at a higher rate than other generations" (Castillo, 2015, p. 4). Millennial's parents and governmental safety regulations had sheltered them from harm's way (DeBard, 2004). With the sheltering of the Millennials, DeBard (2004) stated that "75% of them share their parents' beliefs and values, thus requiring structure at work or in their personal lives (p. 1). As Millennials aged, their affiliations with charities and values for giving back become stronger as handed down from their parents, who continued to volunteer in their retirement. As expected, Millennials would likely pass their values onto their children.

Bucic, Harris, and Arli (2012) declared, "Millennials account for sufficient purchasing power to have a significant current and future impact on world economies, and are accordingly the most powerful consumer group in the marketplace" (p. 114). As the number of Baby Boomers decreased, the market proportion of Millennials would increase in number, as well as the working population. As Millennials gained in purchasing power, marketing managers increased their attention to targeting this attractive and lucrative segment. Establishing new advertising and marketing strategies to better reach Millennials was imperative and would continue to be a priority for years. As the Millennial generation's economic power increased, so does the power of their values, which were likely to influence organizations to adopt a CRM mission.

Generation Z as Consumers

Generation Z was a rapidly emerging cohort of consumers. "Gen Z influences 94 percent of household purchases, and it's confirmed: marketers need to start taking the next generation of power consumers seriously" (Hulyk, 2015, p. 34). Gen Z, roughly defined as those born since 1998, was the first generation born into a digital world. They were considered global and borderless, and they were the most ethnically diverse generation, yet. Dupont, 2015 stated, "This next generation of trendsetters, representing more than 25% of the US population, and two billion globally, has a spending power of $40 billion in the US. Gen Z is already beginning to put its stamp on the world" (p. 19).

Gen Z were known to be even more socially engaged than Gen Y; therefore, marketers will need to communicate in new ways, and CRM campaigns will need to become even more multi-channel to include hashtag social media, Vine, Instagram, Twitter, streaming video, and Quick Response (QR) codes to reach this generation who have "instant access to content through their mobile devices" (Dupont, 2015, p. 19). Generation Z sought honesty, transparency, and authenticity in business, where "entrepreneurship means an opportunity to do something good for the world, following examples set by organizations such as Feed My Starving Children and TOMS Shoes" (Dupont, 2015, p. 19).

Generation Z found power in influence, as they were influenced by public figures to who they can relate; they had a high regard for influence amongst themselves. Gen Z "are influential in the vast majority of their household's purchasing decisions" (Hulyk, 2015, p. 34). Consequently, this evolving cohort of consumers would continue to be a target for marketer's outreach efforts, as they matured, and future research conducted regarding their purchase behavior.

Like Millennials, as Generation Z gained in purchasing power, marketing managers would need to increase their attention to targeting this attractive and lucrative segment. Establishing new advertising and marketing strategies to better reach Generation Z was imperative and would continue to be a priority in the 21st Century. The value of market segmentation for CRM campaigns was critical for the efficiency and effectiveness of the campaign's success. There was little written about or researched on the nuances of CRM consumers and their segmentation. Perhaps because sponsors continued to utilize their segmentation plans for products rather than tailoring marketing efforts towards CRM consumers for CRM campaign products, marketers have become complacent with the success they enjoyed with CRM campaigns.

Social Media

Marketing communications has taken over social media, and social media has become a major component of CRM campaigns. In light of the social awareness of Millennials and Generation Z, it would only make sense that CRM has embraced social media, as Millennials and Generation Z are notably active with Facebook, Pinterest, Twitter, and Instagram. Campaigns have been launched using the creative social media to engage consumers and align a brand with a social cause to develop brand loyalty (Furlow, 2011). Proctor and Gamble's "Dawn Saves Wildlife," had a Facebook page with over 330,000 'likes.' Consumers were driving the communication through social media. "While Dawn is the driving factor behind the program's success, it is ultimately the passion for wildlife conservation that drives the consumer" (Furlow, 2011, p. 63).

Target® developed a two-week campaign that took place around Super Bowl and Valentine's Day called "Super Love Sender." Users were able to select interactive Valentine's Day cards and select one of five preselected charities that would receive a portion of Target's financial donation in the process. No donation amount was required from the user. This successful campaign raised $490,000. "The big winner of the viral campaign was Target, which received 169,000 new Facebook fans as a result of the campaign" (Furlow, 2011, p. 63). Walmart's 2010

'Lend a Paw' campaign featured a Facebook page that promoted the partnership between Walmart and the ASPCA. The campaign resulted in thousands of likes and attracted the attention of consumers aligned to the ASPCA cause.

With social media's popularity, marketers can take part in an active community and connect with consumers at the consumer's convenience and in a creative manner (Furlow, 2011). Communication was instantaneous with use of information technology and social media. The combination of GPS location and target marketing could be used to persuade a potential consumer to make a purchase based on emotion and the 'feel good' value. If Macy's wanted to sell New Balance sneakers, and the consumer had the Macy's app downloaded to their phone, it was possible the Macy's app included location data so Macy's knew the consumer's location. Macy's could push an ad to the consumer that read, "Will donate 10% of sale to breast cancer research for the next three hours." Macy's may also know the consumer had donated to breast cancer; if they had data in a marketing cloud database.

A CRM campaign promoted via social media could result in more contributions and revenue, but the opposite was also true. If a firm did something that hurt rather than helped, and the action was reported on social media, the outcome could result in fewer contributions and revenue. Marketing managers would want to focus their research efforts on rapidly changing social media and the use of cell phone apps, while formulating their marketing mix to reach Millennial and Generation Z consumers.

Affiliation

This study explored the relationship between consumer affiliation with charities and consumer purchase preference for CRM campaign products. The findings would motivate sponsors to take a second look at their marketing segmentation plan for CRM campaigns and integrate findings from this study into marketing of CRM campaign products. Consumer affiliation involved many aspects, but for this research study the consumer's experience as an employee, a volunteer, a donor, and a beneficiary associated with charities was studied in-depth. In addition, the consumer reported the affiliation of immediate family and close friends, just as they had reported their own affiliation, to account for the impact of family values on the consumer.

Affiliation is defined as, "the consumer and the consumer's immediate family and close friends who currently or in the past were an employee of, a volunteer with, a beneficiary of, or a donor (product or money) to a charity" (Kuntz-Azan, 2016). Affiliation was inclusive of engagement, involvement and relationships with charities. There was a tendency to segment the market for CRM campaign products based on the attributes of consumers in general or those consumers likely to purchase in the traditional product category. The attribute of affiliation with a charity could have reduced a better segmentation plan and required advertising and marketing efforts different from those in already in use.

Although affiliation may not be the single most important attribute to best attract consumers to CRM campaigns, it could greatly contribute to the success of CRM campaigns for the charities involved and the sponsors looking to capitalize on their social investment. Affiliation brings to light identification of who was the consumer of CRM campaign products. Who were those who needed or wantd CRM campaign products to simply and primarily support the specific charity or any charity associated with the CRM campaign product, when purchasing the specific product or a similar product from the product category. This study investigated the consumer's relationship with charities, affiliation, and attempts to measure the strength of the consumer's affiliation and its relationship to purchase preference for CRM campaign products.

Employees

An employee was defined as, "One who is working at a charity for wages" (Kuntz-Azan, 2016). Working for a charity was an experience with benefits unlike those received from working at a for-profit organization. Employees of charities see the good they are doing, the difference they are making, and the impact of their efforts. Such benefits may have kept employees from leaving charities for higher pay, more responsibility, greater promotion potential, and better benefits. The relationship between employees and the charity's volunteers added a different dynamic than that of co-workers. Volunteers were at the organization because they want to be, not because they needed to make a living.

When parents or siblings work for a charity, one learns about the satisfaction achieved with what they did, the pride they had for the mission of the charity, and feelings about giving to others. Families who worked at charities shared their vision of work with their children, hoping to open a new avenue for their future. The individual who worked for a charity personally saw the needs of the charity and desperate needs of those they helped. Both experiences, family and self and working at a charity, impacted the affiliation one had with charity work and giving, thus impacting a preference to purchase CRM campaign products.

Volunteers

A volunteer was defined as, "someone who gives their time to a charity" (Kuntz-Azan, 2016). Volunteering was a charitable act of kindness from an individual who generously gives of their time. An individual's commitment of their time to volunteering was, in part, related to their current living status, including their spouse and children, as well as their employment, career status, and personal commitments. Even with busy lives, many made the time to volunteer, regardless of their personal and work situations. "In today's unstable economy, most non-profit organizations suffering from lack of financial resources rely heavily on a volunteer workforce" (Bang, Ross, & Reio, 2013, p. 96).

As is often said, time is money; this is certainly the case for charities. The time volunteers spent helping the charity serve its mission was a savings to the charity and a key factor in its growth. Without volunteerism, most charities would not have survived or served their mission; they were vulnerable without monetary donations from individuals, corporations, and grants. Although corporate sponsors of CRM campaigns gave generously to charities, it was volunteers who spent hours each week working the day-to-day operations of a charity to provide a service or product to those they helped. Bang et al. (2013) agreed that, "Committed and enthusiastic volunteers are a valuable asset to non-profit organizations (p. 96).

Sherraden, Lough, and McBride (2008) declared, "The 21st Century is witnessing an unprecedented expansion of volunteering and service, domestically and internationally, both in numbers of volunteers and sponsoring organizations" (p. 395). Bang et al. (2013) found that, "Based on the Bureau of Labor Statistics of the US Department of Labor (2010), about 63.4 million people performed volunteer work" in 2010 (p. 96).

The question many asked was, "How are volunteers motivated, when employees are not." Volunteers are not paid; employees are paid and have benefits. Bang et al. (2013) shared that, "Given that volunteer activity does not involve monetary rewards, motivation is an indispensable factor to consider when trying to understand why individuals volunteer and what sustains this type of behavior" (p. 99). Bang et al. also explained that a "volunteer organizational commitment can be considered as one's attitude toward an organization related to the willingness to dedicate a significant time and effort to the organization without monetary compensation" (Bang et al., 2013, p. 97).

Although individuals may never know the real difference between the motivation of volunteers and employees, most would say volunteers were intrinsically motivated by the volunteering itself, the people with whom they come in contact, the feeling they had from their volunteer experience, and the trust they had in the charity. "Trust is critically important in relationships between donors and non-profits and is the foundation for voluntary association within the nonprofit sector" (Tonkiss & Passey, 2001, p. 257). Volunteering was something volunteers did not have to do; it was something they wanted to do. Most importantly, volunteers continued to volunteer, many throughout their lives, serving as role models and motivating their family and friends to volunteer.

Perhaps the volunteer's deep commitment to volunteering came from the guiding principles of their lives, their search for new friends, or simply their need to socialize. Volunteering provided those and many other opportunities. According to Bang et al. (2013),

Social exchange theory suggests that voluntary relationships of individuals are induced by the exchange of rewards that the individuals

expect to happen. Individuals strive to incur
the lowest cost, benefit the most of rewards
and then create a likelihood of developing
social relationships with someone or an entity
on the perceived possible outcomes" (p. 97).

Choi and Kim (2011) studied psychological effects and how donations of time and money related to social engagement, identity, and support. Folse, Niedrick, and Grau (2010) suggested motivation was based on trust and the social exchange theory where "reciprocity plays a central role" (p. 303).

Although volunteering at a charity was not typically a requirement in life, often times there was pressure on young and old to volunteer from a variety of sources. Colleges required students to volunteer to earn credit, in part or in full for a college course, to enhance the college's reputation, and/or to create a competitive advantage over other colleges. Many teenagers were advised to volunteer by family, friends, and high school counselors because college admissions officers and employers look for young people who have volunteered time in high school, sports activities, and other organizations such as Boy

Scouts, Girl Scouts, and/or church groups. Baby Boomers and seniors were commonly pressured to volunteer by friends and family, to get them out of their homes and involved with others.

Pressure could also generate from within – volunteers trying to meet their own expectations to volunteer – and from others in their family or their close friends who volunteer. Children who grew up in homes where their parents worked for or volunteered for a charity learned through parental role models that volunteering was a good thing and perhaps was expected by parents. If an individual grew up receiving benefits from charities to survive in hard times, the individual may have felt grateful and want to give to others, in turn. Families that donated money, food, and clothing, and household items passed on their volunteer values to their children. Growing up in a family highly affiliated with charities in various ways purposefully imprinted their values for charitable giving to their children. As children grew up, they inherently knew what was expected of them as a member of their family. "Those within the same nuclear or extended family often think, behave, and live similarly. Of all social groups, the family probably exerts more influence on individuals than those of other groups to which the person belongs" (Alreck & Settle, 2004, p. 23). The affiliation of one's family to charities was related to an individual's affiliation with charities, which in turn, impacted the individual's preference to purchase a CRM campaign product.

Donors

A donor is, "… someone who has given money, food, clothing or household items to a charity" (Kuntz-Azan, 2016). Donors were motivated to participate for both socio-emotional reasons and economic reasons. Taylor (2012) explained, "If non-profit organizations want to deepen their level of engagement with donors, they must first understand donors as unique individuals with individual charitable giving motivations or reasons for giving" (p. 144). Making the decision to donate to a charity rather than selling unwanted items at a garage sale or through Craig's List, was a choice to give to others through a charitable organization. Monetary donations may be an easy way to give to charitable organizations or to give to a special cause that was important to the donor. Donations of money, food, clothing or household items were tax deductible and an incentive for working adults.

Taylor (2012) suggested, "The more a donor identifies with an organization, the higher the level of charitable giving, and the more satisfied a donor is with the relationship with a nonprofit, the higher the level of charitable giving" (p. 14). Smith and Alcorn (1991) agreed, "The prosocial behavior literature argues that the physically closer the recipient to the potential donor, the more likely it is that the potential donor will engage in some form of helping behavior" (p. 23). Baruch and Sang (2012) found engagement, such as operationalized volunteering, was a significant mediating factor for donating behavior: "Engagement and involvement with charities is a factor in predicting future intention to donate. This can be due to the association between engagement and identification" (p. 808).

Arnett et al. (2003) asserted, "Identity theory posits that people have several 'identities,' that is, self-conceptions or self-definitions in their lives. Identity theory suggests that identities are arranged hierarchically and that salient identities are more likely to affect behavior than those that are less important" (p. 89). Philanthropic psychology was an emerging field based on what motivates donors to give, and much of their motivation was found to be from identity saliency. Arnett et al.'s (2003) study found alumni who were active on campus in various groups and organizations were more likely to donate to their university as alumni, because they more closely identified with the university. The alumni whose identity was more salient and stronger gave more than those students whose affiliation with the university was less salient. In other words, alumni who were not involved with organizations and activities on campus were less likely to donate to the university when they became alumni.

Bang et al. (2013) opined, "Given that volunteer activity does not involve monetary rewards, motivation is an indispensable factor to consider when trying to understand why individuals volunteer and what sustains this type of behavior" (p. 99). Donations like working for a charity and volunteering could be imprinted on children from their families' actions and values. Children respected their role models and learn from them as to what was good and what was bad. Donors may feel their families and friends expected them to donate unwanted items or money to charities and put pressure on them to do so. Consequently, donors may have had such expectations for themselves and put pressure on themselves to donate. The act of donation was a component of affiliation impacting the individual's preference for purchasing a CRM campaign product.

Beneficiaries

A beneficiary was someone who has received something of value from a charity such as scholarships, help with housing or utilities, hospice care, or room and board at a Ronald McDonald House (Kuntz-Azan, 2016). Being or knowing a beneficiary could have created pressure or guilt to volunteer, essentially to pay back what they or others had received. There were times in everyone's life that they needed help – whether from family and friends or from a charitable organization. Asking for help could be a humbling experience a struggling family or individual goes through from no fault of their own. Charities asked few questions of those they helped;

they freely offer food and water, shelter and material goods, counseling and legal advice to help those in need through the rough spots in their lives. Although not asking for anything in return, charities may see those they helped return in the future to help others. Those who have been a beneficiary of a charity may place pressure or guilt on themselves to give back through donations or volunteering their time. They may have believed their (later) success would not have happened without the help of the charity. Family members that shared in their experience may expect the beneficiary to contribute in some way as the family had, placing pressure on the individual as well. The experience of being a beneficiary of a charity stays with recipients, likely linking the charitable experience of yesterday to one's charitable gifts and actions of tomorrow. Consumers whose family and friends had received help from charities were more likely to affiliate with charities. "Those within the same nuclear or extended family often think, behave, and live similarly. Of all social groups, the family probably exerts more influence on individuals than those of other groups to which the person belongs" (Alreck & Settle, 2004, p. 23).

Guiding Principles/Personal Rules

Each individual has personal rules and/or guiding principles to live by. Perhaps a deep commitment to volunteering comes from the guiding principles/personal rules of our lives, our search for new friends, or simply our need to socialize. Individuals had different senses of urgency when volunteering, donating, and helping other people in need. Volunteers lived their lives with varying levels of accountability for self, and how they expected other people to hold themselves accountable. Some people were more generous than others, demonstrating different levels of care and kindness, trust in others, as well as trust in self. Some people found it easy to set goals and achieve them, while other people do not feel being charitable was a priority. Employees have experienced working with peers who provide varying levels of approachability, organization, and intrinsic attractiveness. Each individual varies in level of importance to be held in esteem and be respected. Guiding principles/ personal rules vary from one individual to the next.

These principles/rules develop from experiences, young and old, alone or with family and friends, good ones and bad, memorable and not, some worth forgetting and some unforgettable.

Purchase Preference

Purchase preference involved the consumer's preferences when faced with a purchase decision. When contemplating the purchase of a product, consumers choose to purchase or not to purchase an item at a specific point. Consumers also decided to buy one product over another or one product over a substitute product. Some products were attached to a time sensitive sale or offer and yet, other products may have been linked to a CRM campaign that may have made the purchase decision more complicated. Some purchases were linked to the timeliness of the consumer's need for the product whereas others were linked to the consumer's access to funds (cash or credit). Consequently, making the decision to purchase immediately, delay a purchase, or not purchase at all can be linked to many different factors.

Syckman, Bloom, and Blazing (2004) explained, "Past research has shown that consumers have favorable attitudes toward companies that support a cause and that these attitudes have the potential to positively impact purchase decisions" (p. 13). Whereas another study found "CRM campaigns did not affect some of their respondents purchasing because they buy only on the basis of price, product quality, or convenience" (Webb & Mohr, 1998, p. 230). Although "a substantial, viable, and identifiable market segment exists that considers a company's level of social responsibility in its purchase decisions," that market may not prefer CRM purchases specifically (Mohr, Webb, & Harris, 2001, p. 69). Marketing managers customarily used purchase behaviors in making strategic marketing decisions. Purchase behaviors and decisions emanated from branding, emotions, economics, price, and quality. These and other factors entered into the consumer's evaluation of the variables of a CRM purchase.

Much of the academic research had turned to the nuances of CRM and provided insights into the outcomes related to such a strategy. Baghi and Gabrielli's (2013) results revealed,

… significant interaction between awareness of for-profit and charitable non-profit brands in defining consumers' willingness to pay for the cause related product and the key impact of awareness of the two partner brands on the likelihood that consumers will make a purchase" (p. 13).

Similarly, Pracejus, and Olsen (2002) noted CRM was similar to brand alliances because CRM links a brand to the charity. Therefore, CRM partnerships with strong compatibility could show improved performance such as increased consumer attitudes toward the brand and firm, and a higher likelihood of purchase by the consumer.

Syckman, Bloom and Blazing (2004) explained, "Past research has shown that consumers have favorable attitudes toward companies that support a cause and that these attitudes have the potential to positively impact purchase decisions" (p. 13). Nguyen (2015) posited, "A high price can have a negative influence on consumer perception of companies supporting CRM campaigns, especially commercial companies. Furthermore, a sensitivity analysis showed that, under the influence of price, consumers with low altruistic attitudes tend to have more negative evaluations of cause related products than those with high altruistic attitudes" (p. 177). Strahilevitz and Myers (1998) observed, "In 1994, in the United States, charitable giving in the form of monetary donations on the part of the individuals, corporations, and foundations totaled $130 billion. Clearly, there is some value associated with acts of altruism, otherwise people would not be contributing" (p. 435). Acts of altruism have continued to increase. "In 2010, 41% of Cone's survey respondents had bought a product associated with a cause over the past year, up from 20% of respondents in 1993" (Eikenberry, 2013, p. 290).

Webb and Mohr's (1998) study found "CRM campaigns did not affect some of their respondents purchasing because they buy only on the basis of price, product quality, or convenience" (p. 230). Monroe (1974) posited, "Much of the early price research focused on the price-quality relationship, and initially considered situations when the only differential information available to respondents was price" (p. 42). Monroe (1974) further stated, "The understanding of the role price plays in the purchase decision process requires an understanding of the information the buyer brings to the purchase situation" (p. 42). For CRM campaign products, it might be said the charity was a feature of quality. A well-known, well-regarded charity might have been seen by consumers as a high-quality attribute of the CRM campaign product. Strahilevitz and Myers (1998) stated, "Linking purchases with charitable donations can be an effective marketing tool. Despite the increased use of charity-linked promotions, few investigations have examined the factors that influence the effectiveness of this tactic" (p. 434).

Purchase preference involved the consumer's preference when faced with a purchase decision. A basic purchase decision would be to buy an item or not to buy the item at a particular time. This decision may be based on the availability of money or credit, how much the product was needed at this point, competing demands for money, if not buying the product will result in a higher price later, or the product not being available later. When a consumer was faced with a purchase decision for the same item linked to a donation to a cause/charity (a CRM campaign product), the dynamics of the consumer's decision and preference became more complicated, including thinking of the opportunity to give to others, how the consumer felt about the cause/charity, the expiration of the CRM offer, and who the CRM sponsor is that is offering the CRM campaign product. "Emotions can influence consumer attitudes; this is also true for consumer response to CRM campaigns. One of the ample informational cues that humans integrate into their purchase decisions in this scope are assumptions about a firms' motivation to engage in CRM" (Moosemayer & Fuljahn, 2013, p. 205). Consequently, in an economic exchange, the consumer must be willing to pay for the CRM campaign product typically priced higher than competitive products. Folse, Niedrich and Grau (2010) wrote, "Consumers are inspired to participate in CRM campaigns for both socio-emotional reasons and economic reasons. Consumers expect firms to fulfill their donation obligation to the charity. More importantly, consumers evaluate the CRM offer as an economic transaction" (p. 295). Although CRM was viewed as an economic transaction, consumers balanced price with many product, manufacturer, retailer, CRM sponsor, and charity attributes. Determining the most effective ways to segment and create target markets for CRM campaigns would present an understanding of how the role affiliation plays was related to the purchase preference process. This required a keen perception of the information the consumer brought to the purchase setting. Marketing managers customarily used purchase behavior in their strategic marketing decisions, yet understanding the relationship between affiliation and purchase preference, and how that relationship contributes to market segmentation and targeting had yet to be clearly defined.

Brands

Sponsor, charity, and product brands contributed to the consumer's decision to purchase a CRM campaign product. Baghi and Gabrielli's (2013) research revealed a "significant interaction between awareness of for-profit and non-profit brands in defining consumers' willingness to pay for the cause related product and the key impact of awareness of the two partner brands on the likelihood that consumers will make a purchase" (p. 13). Consequently, "Linking a brand with a cause can trigger more positive attitude on the brand and the cause it supports and also affects purchase decisions" (Anuar, Omar, & Mohamad, 2013, p. 71). Fournier (1998) "argues for the validity of the relationship proposition in the consumer-brand context, including a debate as to the legitimacy of the brand as an active relationship partner" supporting the significance of consumer brand bonds (p. 343). Engagement and involvement could be used to predict purchase preference. Grau and Folse (2007) discussed how consumer brand involvement represented the consumer's motivation to make a CRM purchase in an environment where "a multitude of CRM campaigns compete for the limited number of socially conscious consumers" (p. 19).

There were types of relationships consumers formed with brands. Consumers that showed a high level of brand engagement had been labeled as 'influencers.' Those consumers refered their favorite products and brands to others in today's tech-savvy and connected society. Other influencers included celebrity and social media stars, executives, journalists, and bloggers who influenced consumers through Tweets, Instagram, Facebook, YouTube, and other social networking outlets. Evaluating the attributes of the brands involved in a CRM campaign and the most appropriate consumer segments for marketing the brands greatly enhanced the potential of a successful CRM campaign.

Fournier's (1998) research discussed the types of relationships that consumers formed with brands. Fournier's research also "argues for the validity of the relationship proposition in the consumer-brand context, including a debate as to the legitimacy of the brand as an active relationship partner and empirical support for the phenomenological significance of consumer brand bonds" (p. 343). "Linking a brand with a cause can trigger more positive attitude on the brand and the cause it supports and also affects purchase decisions (Anuar et al., 2013, p. 71). Similarly, Thomas, Fraedrich and Mullen (2001) stated, "Studies of composite branding alliances found that greater compatibility leads to greater success. These studies suggest that consumer attitudes towards brands are increased when compatibility is high" (p. 114). When a supplier had a well-known brand for the product they supplied to a CRM organization, the organization would require, via contract, that the supplier participated in CRM campaign products offer branding of both the CRM sponsor and the charity. These two brands could be favored by the consumer, or neither can be favored, or one can be favored and the other not. Each brand contributed to the consumer's decisions to choose the CRM campaign product to purchase. "Linking a brand with a cause can trigger more positive attitude on the brand and the cause it supports and also affects purchase decisions" (Anuar et al., 2013, p. 71). The organization could have also reviewed their suppliers to see which ones were supporting a charity and/or engaged in CRM. This would allow the CRM organization to advertise that they prefered to partner with CRM suppliers.

Economic Factors

A CRM purchase was an economic exchange involving three parties: the consumer, the sponsor, and the charity. Although the addition of the charitable contribution was an attractive feature to many, its presence complicated the consumer's evaluation of this economic exchange. In an economic exchange, the consumer must be willing to pay for the CRM campaign product typically priced higher than competitive products. Folse et al. (2010) asserted, "Consumers are inspired to participate in CRM campaigns for both socio-emotional reasons and economic reasons. Consumers expect firms to fulfill their donation obligation to the non-profit organization. More importantly, consumers evaluate the CRM offer as an economic transaction" (p. 295). Although CRM was viewed as an economic transaction, consumers balanced price with other product, manufacturer, retailer, for-profit sponsor, and charity attributes.

Economic trends included purchasing power, inflation, and recession. "Consumer confidence reflects consumer perceptions of future economic trends. As such, confidence indices constitute a convenient and useful tool for predicting future household spending" (Kwan & Cotsomitis, 2004, p. 136). When income was high relative to the cost of living, consumers were likely to spend more money on wants rather than needs (Lamb, Hair, & McDaniel, 2013). The way consumers perceived economic trends and their perceptions related to their purchasing behavior was vitally important to marketers. Taylor's (2011) findings suggested, "Further research is needed on relationships that are economic in nature for non-profits, thereby filling a gap, or an apparent variable that has possibly been ignored, in the past" (p. 203). Therefore, an understanding of consumer expectations of CSR should be noted when creating CRM campaigns.

Emotions

Often, a purchase decision was more than a choice between products and the products' features and attributes. A final decision may have been based solely on emotions. An emotional decision may have been well thought out and reasoned or it may have been an automatic response to an emotional trigger. An emotional trigger may or may not be weighed with the price when the purchase was for a CRM campaign product. For some consumers, price did not matter when faced with a purchase decision that helped others as the case with a CRM campaign product. "In the relational exchange of values, consumers invest an emotional element" (Taylor, 2012, p. 20). Overall, "Emotions can influence consumer attitudes" and this is also "true for consumer responses to CRM campaigns," (Moosemayer & Fuljahn, 2013, p. 205).

Price

Setting the price for a CRM campaign product was a complex process to ensure the sponsor made a fair profit, the charity received a fair donation, and the consumer paid a fair price. Consumers may notice some CRM campaign products were no more expensive than similar products or the same product without or before the CRM campaign, but at other times believed the CRM campaign product's price was inflated to cover the charitable donation. Only the sponsor knew the cost of the CRM campaign product and impact of sales volume on product costs. The charity and the sponsor were in a contractual agreement for the agreed upon donation amount.

Monroe (1974) posited, "Much of the early price research focused on the price-quality relationship, and initially considered situations when the only differential information available to respondents was price" (p. 42). Monroe (1974) further stated, "The understanding of the role price plays in the purchase decision process requires an understanding of the information the buyer brings to the purchase situation" (p. 42). Nguyen (2015) affirmed,

> *"A high price can have a negative influence on consumer perceptions of companies supporting CRM campaigns, especially commercial companies. Furthermore, a sensitivity analysis shows that under the influence of price, consumers with low altruistic attitudes tend to have more negative evaluations of cause related products than those with high altruistic attitudes" (p. 177).*

Price was an important factor for consumers and in relation to the product quality and brand, the CRM donation practice, and the value the consumer placed on the sponsor brands and charitable organization.

Quality

Quality has long been a factor related to product price. The ratio of quality for price was a sign of value to consumers. For CRM campaigns, the charity could serve as a feature of quality for consumers contemplating the purchase of a CRM campaign product. A well-known, well regarded charity with good branding was easily perceived as a quality institution and their reputation served as a measure of quality for the purchase of a CRM campaign product. Consequently, the choice of the charity reflects on the CRM campaign product, as well as the CRM campaign's success.

Demographic Attributes

Demographic attributes included gender, age, living status, number of children living in household, race, length of time lived in the Tampa Bay area, education, household income, and career status.

They also include psychographic questions regarding personal rules society lives by, and values. Demographic and psychographic questions were used to classify data, compare the results by classification, profile the respondents and determine the data's impact on purchase preference characteristics and attitudes. Demographics were important when investigating variables because marketers create key-customer segments based on variables that can be used to identify, enumerate and reach the right consumers at the right time. Alreck and Settle (2004) stated, "demographics can be used to identify segments of people who are both identifiable and behave in similar ways" (p. 24). To reach the preferred segments, marketers seek to identify the most attractive demographic niches (Strauss & Frost, 2014). By having a clearer understanding of the relationship between charity affiliation and purchase preference for CRM campaign products, organizations could tailor their marketing campaigns to their specific target market.

Limited Research

Much of the academic research has turned to the nuances of CRM and provided insights into the outcomes related to such a strategy. Research indicated that "Despite the increased use of charity linked promotions, few investigations have examined the factors that influence the effectiveness of CRM" (Strahilevitz & Myers, 1998, p. 434). Liston-Heyes and Liu (2013) stated, "While there is considerable work on CRM from a corporate angle, very little has been done from a non-profit perspective, particularly in terms of developing a conceptual and theoretical understanding of the strategies available to non-profit managers" (p. 1974).

Runte, Basil, and Deshpande (2009) concurred, "Very little research has addressed the impact of CRM on managerial issues relevant to non-profit organizations. Engagement of participants in the CRM process has been the focus of recent research, although considerable knowledge gaps remain" (p. 257). In addition, Taylor (2012) found, "Further research is needed on relationships that are economic in nature for non-profit organizations, thereby filling a gap, or an apparent variable that has possibly been ignored, in the past" (p. 203). Taylor (2012) also suggested, "There is a need for research on market segmentation for identifying relationships that influence behaviors" (p. 10). Fornier (1998) explained, "Although the relationship metaphor dominates contemporary marketing thought and practice, surprisingly little empirical work has been conducted on relational phenomena in the consumer products domain, particularly at the level of the brand" (p. 343). This exploratory research study was designed to investigate the affiliation of potential consumers of CRM campaign products and their purchase preferences to find the presence of their relationship.

CHAPTER THREE:

METHODOLOGY

This chapter was divided into the following subsections: (a) research design, (b) sampling and respondents (c) instrumentation, (d) cause-related marketing campaigns (e) "your chosen CRM" (f) purchase preference and CRM campaign products (g) methodological assumptions and limitations (h) procedures, and (i) data processing and analysis.

The research design section consisted of a research model, the research question, and the hypothesis. The sampling and respondents section consisted of the population and sample, sampling method, response rate, and respondent profile. The instrumentation section detailed the age qualifying question, variables, survey measurements, respondent demographics, respondent affiliation (employment, volunteering, donations, beneficiary), and the respondent's immediate family and close friends (employment, volunteering, donations, beneficiary).

The CRM campaigns section consisted of the importance of a CRM campaign product, confidence in CRM donation practices, most desirable, and most undesirable CRM donation practices, CRM campaign product pricing, and CRM donation practices. The "your chosen CRM" section consists of, "your chosen CRM's charity," and "your chosen CRM's" sponsor. The purchase preference and CRM campaign products section explored the research study's participant's feelings about four specific CRM campaigns on eleven bipolar attributes using a 7-point Likert scale. The methodological assumptions and limitations section discussed generalizability, response rate, number of observations for affiliation, inability to contact non-respondents, time constraints, and potential flaws within on-line data collection methods. The procedures section discussed survey instrument feedback from a panel of experts, survey administration, and statistical tests. The final section, data processing and analysis, discussed sequence of the research study events, the use of numeric data to break down affiliation and purchase preference into groups, principal components' analysis (PCA) of the response categories, and the use of SPSS computer-based quantitative analysis software.

Research Design

For this study, quantitative research methods were used to collect data, investigate the relationship between charity affiliation and purchase preference from CRM campaign products, and to test the hypothesis. The exploratory nature of this study and the new variable affiliation, were best served by the advantages of a quantitative approach. These quantitative advantages included the ability to statistically analyze the reliability and validity of affiliation and to identify any variables needing further study. Quantitative numerical responses also allowed statistical analyses needed to conduct frequency and regression analyses. Regression analysis was conducted to explore the relationship between affiliation and purchase preference. A thorough analysis of the new variable – affiliation – was found to be of particular value to this study, academic marketing literature stream, and for future research.

Primary quantitative research for this study involved the use of an online survey. Online surveys were able to be distributed, completed, and a data file created in a short amount of time at a lower cost. Online surveys were also convenient for respondents. Respondents completed the survey in private at a time convenient for them. There was a feeling of anonymity for respondents when the researcher and respondents' colleagues were not watching the respondents complete the survey (paper and pencil survey administration).

Research Model

This research study was based on two constructs: respondent affiliation with a charity and respondent purchase preference for CRM campaign products. Many aspects of a research study respondent's life could have motivated the respondent to become affiliated with a charity. In this study, the respondent's immediate family and close friends were expected to be a driving force behind the respondents choosing to affiliate with charities and their purchase preference for CRM products.

The motivation for a respondent to affiliate with a charity was operationalized as immediate family members and close friends becoming role models based upon their own affiliation with charities. For instance, family members and close friends who, at the time of this research study or in the past, have volunteered at, been employed at, have donated to, and/or have been beneficiaries of a charity serve as role models for the respondents, have expectations for the respondents, and put pressure on the respondents to affiliate with charities.

The higher the affiliation with charities for the respondent's immediate family and close friends, the higher the family and friend's expectations for the respondent; the higher the pressure put on the respondent, the higher the respondent's affiliation was expected to be in this study. The affiliation of, expectations of, and pressure from immediate family members and close friends was expected to motivate respondents to become affiliated with charities (see Figure 2).

Immediate Family and Close Friends Affiliation	⟹	Respondent Affiliation
(volunteering at, being employed at, donating to, being a beneficiary of a charity)		(volunteering at, being employed at, donating to, being a beneficiary of a charity)

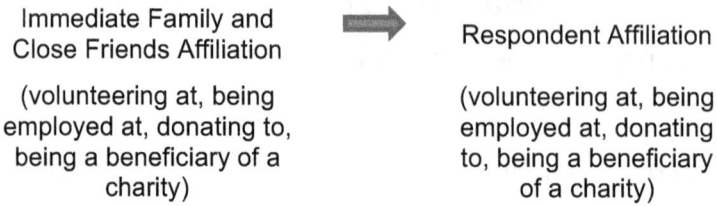

Figure 2 - Research Model for Affiliation (Kuntz-Azan, 2016)

Respondent affiliation was based upon the respondent's personal experience volunteering, being employed at, donating to, and being a beneficiary of a charity. Therefore, the respondents' personal affiliation was measured on the same attributes as their immediate family members and close friends.

The relationship between respondent affiliation and respondent purchase preference for CRM campaign products was the focus of this study. The stronger one's affiliation with a charity, the more likely the individual feels strongly about the charity's mission, needs, and impact. These stronger feelings may well result in stronger purchase preferences for CRM campaign products depending on the various attributes of the CRM campaign. Consequently, a respondent's strong affiliation with charities was believed to be related to the respondent preferring to purchase CRM campaign products (see Figure 3).

Immediate Family and
Close Friends Affiliation ➡ Respondent Affiliation

⬇

Purchase Preference

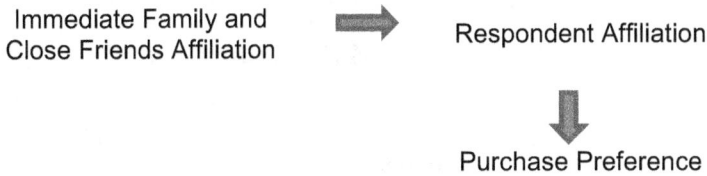

Figure 3 - Research Model for Affiliation and Purchase Preference (Kuntz-Azan, 2016)

Research Question

RQ1: What is the relationship between charity affiliation and purchase preference for cause-related marketing campaign products?

Hypothesis

H_1: There is a relationship between charity affiliation and purchase preference for cause-related marketing campaign products.

H_0: There is not a relationship between charity affiliation and purchase preference for cause-related marketing campaign products.

Sampling and Respondents

Population and Sample

The population for this study was adult consumers age 18 and over. To ensure a full range of responses to affiliation questions were collected, and to avoid overrepresentation and under-representation of the population, two charitable non-profit and three for-profit organizations were chosen to be surveyed. Both charitable non-profit organizations were viable candidates for this research study, as they were both located in the targeted geographic area, they could provide a large database of the types of affiliations being studied (employees, volunteers, donors, and beneficiaries), and their organizational structure was typical to other Tampa Bay area charities.

The three for-profit organizations were also viable candidates for this research study, as they were located in the correct geographic area, and the employees equated to a strong sample size that complimented the charities employee data bases (see Table 2).

Table 2: Organizations and Number of Potential Participants

Organization	Number of Employees	Number of Volunteers
Charity		
"CNPO A"	250	2000
"CNPO B"	9	200
Total	**259**	**2200**
For-profit Organization		
"FPO A"	200	
"FPO B"	200	
"FPO C"	55	
Total	**455**	**0**
Grand Total	**714**	**2200**

Sampling Method

According to Cohen (1992), "In research planning, the investigator needs to know the N necessary to attain the desired power for the specified α and hypothesized ES. N increases with an increase in the power desired, a decrease in the ES, and a decrease in α. For statistical tests involving two or more groups, N as here defined was the necessary sample size for *each* group" (p. 157). The calculation of N needed for each of the eight affiliation groups was 38, totaling 304 (8 x 38) respondents needed for the statistical analysis of the new variable, affiliation.

Cohen's F was initially to be used to conduct ANOVA analysis; however, given the response rate for the individual affiliation questions, composite variables were created to measure affiliation for both the respondent and the respondent's immediate family and close friends. To create composite variables, the researcher assigned numeric scores for each affiliation question and a total score for each respondent's affiliation and for each respondent's immediate family and close friends affiliation. Higher affiliation scores indicated the respondent (or their immediate family and close friends) was highly affiliated with charitable organizations and lower scores indicated lower affiliation. The composite affiliation score was then used to predict purchase preferences using linear regression models. The affiliation predictors in the regression models affected purchase preferences in a similar way suggesting that the responses were valid and could be extrapolated to the wider population from which they were sampled. The distribution of the outcomes was not found to be normally distributed. This could be related to the use of a convenience sample for this study rather than a probability sample from the population. The sample consisted of men and women, 18 years of age, or older who live, work and volunteer in the Tampa Bay area.

A convenience sample was derived from two charitable non-profit organizations and three for-profit organizations. "CNPO A", a charity, consented to distribute the survey to the employees and volunteers. This charity represents approximately 250 employees and 2000 volunteers (See Table 2). "CNPO B" was also approached for consent to conduct the survey with their employees and/or volunteers. This charity represented approximately 9 employees and 200 volunteers (see Table 2).

These two charities were utilized to ensure a number of respondents would have high levels of affiliation given that the survey would be distributed to their employees and volunteers. The value and meaningfulness of this research study lies in the presence of affiliation at various levels in the respondents; consequently, employees and volunteers of these charities were surveyed.

On the other hand, the involvement of for-profit organizations was assumed to provide a greater variation in affiliation, possibly no affiliation, or a weak affiliation to explore the full range of affiliation levels. All employees of these three for-profit organizations were surveyed regardless of position, level, or role in the organization. "FPO A" employs approximately 200 employees, "FPO B" approximately 200 employees, and "FPO C" approximately 55 employees (see Table 2). All employees received the online survey from these three for- profit organizations. Letters from each organization substantiating access and participation in this research study were secured.

Response Rate

Alreck and Settle (2004) stated, "Online surveys, those that collect data by presenting the questionnaire on a web page, share many of the characteristics of mail surveys, including the relatively low response rates which are often only about 5 or 10 percent." The expected response was between 146 and 292 responses (5% of 2914 = 146; 10% of 2914 = 292). This study resulted in 333 usable responses, and the actual response rate was 8.8%. Alreck and Settle (2004) wrote,

"Online surveys are subject to very substantial levels of non-response. Only a fraction of those solicited to visit the website containing the survey questionnaire or who visit it voluntarily or by chance are likely to take the time and exert the effort to complete and submit the questionnaire" (p. 37).

A higher response was expected from the charities, given that the focus of the research was closely aligned with the charity respondents' employment and/or volunteering.

Respondent Profile

Fifty-five (55.6%) percent of the respondents were female. The respondents' average age was 47.5 years. Baby Boomers were best represented at 42%;

Generation X at 28%; Millennials/Generation Y at 26%. Most (84%) of the respondents were Caucasian. Approximately 24% of respondents had earned a high school diploma. A bachelor's degree was earned by 35% of the respondents where as 23.4% had earned a graduate degree (masters or doctorate).

Career status was broken into employed (full or part time), retired (job or no job), career stage, in college and their goals. Respondents who were in college were becoming qualified to improve or change their current career (7.29%), while 1.04% were in college qualifying for their first career. Participants were in their early, mid and late careers, 18.75%, 17.71% and 16.67% respectively. Some participants (12.50%) were working in their second career, 10.42% were working part-time and 39.58% working full-time. While 2.08% of participants were stay at home parents, 6.25% were retired with a part-time job, 6.25% were retired with no job, and 3.13% were unemployed. Annual household income included 33.3% earning between $31,000 and $50,000; 49.8% earning $51,000 to $150,000; and 10.5% earning over $150,000.

Respondents' daily living situation revealed that 22.64% lived alone, 53.77% lived with a spouse, and 13.21 % lived with a roommate, and 10.38% were living with a partner. Respondents reported living with up to 4 children (12.50% answered "1", 8.33% answered "2", 2.08% answered "3" and 1.04% answered "4") in their household on a regular basis while most (76.4%) of respondents had no children in their homes, (Median of 0 children). Respondents lived in the Tampa Bay area on average 22 years whereas respondents averaged working in the Tampa Bay area for 16 years (see Table 6, Chapter Four).

Instrumentation

A self-administered online survey instrument was designed to investigate the relationship between charity affiliation and purchase preference for CRM campaign products. The use of a self-administered survey increases confidentiality, gives respondents a sense of anonymity, and encourages more honest responses; all of which can lead to more valid responses (DeMillo, 2006). The survey instrument consisted of eight sections: (a) demographics (b) your charitable experience (c) charitable experience of your immediate family members and close friends (d) cause-related marketing campaigns (e) "your chosen CRM" (f) "your chosen CRM's charity," (g) "your chosen CRM's sponsor," and (h) purchase preference for CRM campaign products.

Age Qualifying Question

The first question concerned the respondents' current age, which was the only qualifying factor. Respondents were told "only individuals who are 18 and over may participate in this survey." They were then asked: "Are you 18 years or older?" If the respondent answered "yes," then they were told they were qualified and that continuing with the survey was providing consent for the use of their survey information. If the respondent answered "no," they were thanked and the survey was concluded.

Variables

This study measured independent, dependent, and demographic variables.

Independent Variable. "Affiliation" was the independent variable in this study. "The independent variable is the one causing or affecting the other" (Alreck & Settle, 2004, p. 303). To date, affiliation with a charity has not been studied in the academic literature. Webster's Dictionary defines affiliation as: "To closely connect (something or yourself) with or to something (such as a program or organization) as a member or partner" (Merriam-Webster.com). For this study affiliation was defined as "an individual's personal or immediate family and close friends' relationship to a charity as an employee of, a volunteer with, a beneficiary of, or a donor (product or money) to a charity" (Kuntz-Azan, 2016).

For this research study, affiliation was operationalized based on four types of relationships with a charity: (1) employee of, (2) a volunteer with, (3) a beneficiary of, or (4) a donor (product or money) to a charity. These four affiliation types were measured for the respondent and the respondent's immediate family and close friends. Immediate family was defined as "the respondent's spouse, children, parents, and siblings." Close friends were defined as

"Very close relationships that stimulate a consumer to act in a similar manner mirrored by role models in familial relationships." Affiliation was measured with straight forward questions asking for facts about the respondent and the respondent's immediate family and close friend's affiliation with charities. Respondents reported their personal affiliation and recalled the affiliation of their immediate family members and close friends. This resulted in eight measures of affiliation: (1) respondent as an employee, (2) a volunteer, (3) a beneficiary, and (4) a donor, and the respondent's recall of their (5) immediate family members and close friends as employees, (6) volunteers, (7) beneficiaries, and (8) donors.

An employee was one working at a for-profit organization and/or a charity for wages. A volunteer was someone who gives their personal time to a charity. A beneficiary received something of value from a charity such as a scholarship, help with housing or utilities, hospice care, or room and board at a Ronald McDonald House. A donor was someone who has given money, food, and/or clothing and/or household products to a charity. A donor was not someone who has volunteered time.

Dependent Variable. "Purchase preference" was the dependent variable for this study. "The dependent variable is the one being caused or affected" (Alreck & Settle, 2004, p. 303). The Collins Dictionary of Economics defines purchase preference as, "the choices made by consumers as to which products to consume" (as cited in Pass, Davies & Lowes, 2006, p. 316). For this study, consumers reported their preference for a cause-related marketing campaign product from a CRM sponsor based upon the four components of a CRM campaign: the CRM campaign product, the CRM sponsor, the charitable organization and the CRM donation practice.

Cause-related marketing was defined as, "a marketing program that attempts to achieve two goals – improving corporate performance and helping worthy causes by connecting fund raising for the benefit of a cause to the purchase of a firm's products" (Varadarajan & Menon, 1988, p. 58). For example, when a consumer purchases a specific CRM product from such an organization, a donation of proceeds or product were given to the charity. Consequently, a CRM product was defined as something that must be offered by a CRM sponsor to benefit a charity in either proceeds or in kind products. Tom's Shoes was one example of a CRM sponsor with a CRM mission. For each pair of shoes purchased, Tom's gives a pair of shoes away to "Save the Children" (a charity).

For this study, purchase preference did not include buying directly from a charity engaged in a fund-raising event or activity where there was no involvement or relationship with a CRM sponsor. An example of this would be purchasing Girl Scout cookies or a pet, for a fee, from a charity. Respondents were only and specifically asked to report their preference for purchasing a cause-related marketing product from a for-profit organization.

Demographic Variables. Demographics were important when investigating variables because marketers create key-customer segments based on variables that could be used to identify, enumerate, and reach the right consumers at the right time. To reach the preferred segments, marketers should seek to identify the most attractive demographic niches (Strauss & Frost, 2014). By having a clearer understanding of the relationship between charity affiliation and purchase preference for CRM campaign products, organizations tailor their marketing campaigns to their specific market.

Survey Measurements

The survey included sections of questions concerning the respondent's demographics, respondent's affiliation to charities (volunteering, donations, employment, and beneficiary), the respondent's immediate family and close friend's affiliation to charities (volunteering, donations, employment, and beneficiary), cause-related marketing campaigns (importance of CRM campaign product, confidence in CRM donation practices, most undesirable and least undesirable CRM donation practices, and CRM campaign product pricing and CRM donation practices), "your chosen CRM" (your CRM charity and your CRM sponsor), and purchase preference for CRM campaign products.

Respondent Demographics

Demographic questions included gender, age, living status, children living in household, race, length of time lived in the Tampa Bay area, education, household income, and career status. The survey also included psychographic questions regarding personal rules we live by, and values. Demographic and psychographic questions were used to classify data, compare the results by classification, profile the respondents and determine the data's impact on purchase preference characteristics and attitudes. Demographic data collected could contribute to the descriptive statistics of the study and provides insight into future research.

The demographic questions and the methods used for collecting the information included the following.

1.   Gender: Participants chose either "male" or "female."
2.   Age: Participants wrote in their age as of their last birthday.
3.   Living Status: Participants identified their current living status from: "living alone (married, not

married, single, divorced, or widowed);" "living with a spouse (married);" "living with roommate(s), but not a partner;" and "living with a partner (single, divorced, widowed, or not married)." A partner is defined as "one with whom you are in a committed relationship, but not married to."

4. Children: Participants identified the number of children living daily in their household.

5. Race: Participants identified their race from: "Asian," "White/Caucasian," "African American," and "other.

6. Participants identified the number of years they have lived in the Tampa Bay area.

7. Education: Participants identified the highest level of education they have completed from: "High School Diploma," "Associate's Degree," "Bachelor's Degree," "Master's Degree," "Doctorate Degree," or "None of the above."

8. Career Status: Participants identified their current career status from I am: "in college to become qualified for my first career;" "in college to improve my current career or to change careers;" "in my early career;" "in mid-career;" "in

late career;" "working in my second career;"
"working part-time;" "working full-time;" "full-time
military;" "a stay-at-home parent or homemaker;"
"retired with a part-time job;" "retired-no job;" and
"unemployed." Respondents may select all that
apply.

9. Participants identified the number of years they
have worked in the Tampa   Bay area

10. Income: Participants identified total yearly
earned household income before taxes from:
"less than $15,000 a year," "$15,000 to $30,000
a year," "$31,000 to $50,000 a year," "$51,000 to
$75,000 a year," "$76,000 to $150,000 a year,"
and "over $150,000 a year."

11. Guiding Principles/Personal Rules:

Respondents identified the personal rules they
lived by and indicated their level of agreement with
the following statements using a 7-point Likert scale
(1-Strongly Disagree, 4-Neither Agree nor Disagree,
7-Strongly Agree).

Note: The survey instrument (Question 11), is
protected under copyright. Contact Dr. Carolanne

Kuntz Azan: dr.carolannekuntz@yahoo.com and/or
Dr. Sherri Kae at sherrijk@gmail.com, for further
information regarding the Guiding Principles and/or
Personal Rules questions.

Respondent Affiliation

Affiliation questions addressed the
respondents' experience being employed at,
volunteering with, donating to, and being a beneficiary
of a charity. These questions assessed the strength
of the respondents' affiliation to charities.

Cause-Related Marketing Campaigns

In this section of the survey, respondents were
asked questions about the four parts of a CRM
campaign to better understand their purchase
preferences for CRM campaign products. First,
respondents were given the four components of the
campaign to include the: "CRM sponsor," "charity,"
"CRM campaign product," and "CRM donation
practice (amount)." Five CRM campaigns from the
last 2 years were detailed: Unilever and Direct Relief,

Cumberland Farms and the ALS Association, Wendy's and the Dave Thomas Foundation for Adoption, New Balance and the Susan G. Komen Race for Cure, and Gfour Products and the Susan G. Komen Foundation. Respondents were then asked general questions about CRM campaign products and CRM donation practices.

Consumers considered the product itself, the CRM donation practice, the charity, and the CRM sponsor associated with the CRM campaign. The product had many features and qualities to be evaluated by the consumer in addition to the importance of the product's price and features. The consumer may or may not have a history with the charity and the CRM sponsor. Lastly, the CRM donation practice involved the amount to be donated to the charity. The consumer's confidence in the CRM donation practice and their understanding of the amount to be donated were important considerations as well as the relationship of the donation to the price the consumer pays for the CRM campaign product.

Purchase Preference for CRM Campaign Products

Purchase preference for CRM campaign products was a complex decision; however, in this section respondents were asked directly about CRM purchases and their likelihood of making a CRM purchase, how likely they were to seek information on a CRM campaign, choosing between purchasing a CRM and non-CRM campaign product, identifying the deal-breaker among the four components of a CRM campaign, and rank ordering the four components of a CRM campaign. The survey concluded by thanking the respondents for their participation in the study, then Survey Monkey closed.

Methodological Assumptions and Limitations

Limitations of the quantitative survey methodology utilized for this research study included generalizability, response rate, number of observations for affiliation, inability to contact non-respondents, time restraints, and potential flaws within on-line data collection methods. It was not uncommon for generalizability to be a limitation of exploratory research such as this study. The convenience sample, geographic location of the respondents, types of charities, and sample size greatly impact the generalizability. It was expected that the results were generalizable to the culture of other similarly structured organizations, in the Tampa Bay area. The sample consisted of two charitable non-profit organizations and three for-profit organizations located in the Tampa Bay area. Therefore, within the parameters of the research design there were certain limitations on generalizability.

Anonymity and confidentiality for the respondents inherently restricted the researcher to email reminders through the human resources department at the for-profit organization and the charitable non-profit organization. These reminders had to be sent to all respondents and could not be limited or targeted to those who had not yet responded. Consequently, this limitation may well reduce the response rate, thus limiting validity and generalizability. The organizations might have restricted access for survey administration to a limited period of time that did not make it possible for respondents to take the survey during work hours. Such constraints might have limited the respondents' ability to complete the survey at a time convenient for them.

The potential flaws within online data collection methods include the need for a large sample size, low interaction with respondents, and the severity of nonresponse bias. In order to mitigate these potential flaws, the sum of the two non-profit and three for-profit organizations who were sent the on-line survey link equate to 2914 potential respondents. In order to alleviate non-response bias, charitable non-profit and for-profit organizations were chosen to collect the data to avoid overrepresentation and underrepresentation of population.

Procedures

The survey packet consisted of an emailed cover letter with a link to the online survey and the online survey. The cover letter adhered to Argosy University's IRB requirements and included explaining the purpose of the research study and the general content of the survey, introducing the researcher and the researcher's relationship to the study, stating the time required to complete the survey and the open period to access the survey, explaining the importance of the research, ensuring confidentiality, directing the respondent's on how to learn of the outcomes of the research, and providing instructions how to proceed to the survey instrument on Survey Monkey. A link to the survey was provided at the end of the cover letter. The link took the respondent to Survey Monkey to complete the survey online.

Respondents were first asked if they were 18 years of age or older. If the respondent answered positively, a statement of consent appeared. The statement of consent notified the respondent that continuing with the survey meant they were giving their consent for the use of their answers in the research. If the respondent selected "continue to the survey," the first survey question appeared. If the respondent responded negatively to the age question, a thank you note appeared and the survey was closed.

Respondents were unable to stop and return to the survey at a later time. The survey instrument consisted of instructions for each major section and to assist respondents when question styles and/or response formats changed. Sections included (a) demographics (b) your charitable experience (c) charitable experience of your immediate family members and close friends (d) cause-related marketing campaigns (e) "your chosen CRM" (f) "your chosen CRM's charity," (g) "your chosen CRM's CRM sponsor," and (h) purchase preference for CRM campaign products. Questions were developed to cross check strength of affiliation. At the end of the survey, respondents were thanked for their participation.

Feedback from Panel of Experts

To test the reliability of the survey instrument, the researcher administered the initial survey instrument to a panel of five experts. This panel consisted of two business owners in the Tampa Bay area, a recently retired philanthropist and volunteer, a business development representative at a local non-profit organization, and a financial analyst who completed her DBA in 2014, who also created her own survey instrument. The self-administered survey was sent to the panel via e-mail, and the completed surveys were returned to the researcher, via e-mail. This was repeated by sending the same identical surveys to the same panel two weeks later, to see if there were any differences in the respondent's answers. "The reliability coefficient obtained with repetition of an identical measure on a second occasion is called test-retest reliability" (Sekaran, 2003, p. 173).

Cronbach's alpha was a measure of internal consistency, that is, how closely related a set of items were as a group. It was a measure of scale reliability which abstract health psychologists using questionnaires rely heavily upon, as an indicator of scale reliability and internal consistency (Peters, 2014). "Unfortunately, this approach suffers two fundamental problems. First, Cronbach's alpha was both unrelated to a scale's internal consistency and a fatally flawed estimate of its reliability. Second, the approach itself assumes that scale items were repeated measurements, an assumption often violated and rarely desirable. The problems with Cronbach's alpha were easily solved by computing readily available alternatives" (Peters, 2014, p. 1). Therefore, Pearson correlation was utilized. "A correlation coefficient is a number that tells the strength and the direction of a relationship. There were several different correlation statistics, each appropriate for data having a shape or underlying scale. The Pearson r is appropriate for use with scores whose underlying relationship is linear and measured on at least an interval scale" (Steinberg, 2011, p. 432).

Pearson correlation indicate the two scores were highly correlated, which supports a majority of the responses were the same from the first and second survey administrations (see Table 3). The survey had a high test-retest reliability as evidenced by a Pearson correlation coefficient of 92%. The mean scores were also similar on both surveys which suggests that the survey measures what it was expected to measure; the survey was internally valid.

Table 3: Paired Samples Correlations

Paired Samples Correlations				
		N	Correlation	Sig.
Pair 1	Total & Total 2	5	.926	.024

Table 3 shows the correlation between the test and retest reliability values. Correlation of .926 represents a high test-retest reliability. P=.024, less than .05, and hence, significant.

Table 4: Paired Samples Statistics

Paired Samples Statistics

		Mean	N	Std. Deviation	Std. Error Mean
Pair 1	Total	173.60	5	29.280	13.094
	Total 2	171.40	5	31.437	14.059

Table 4 showed the paired sample *t*-test results. The p value is = .699 > .05, and hence, not significant. Table 4 (*t*-test) also showed the means of the before score and the after score were similar (173.60 vs. 171.40). This suggests the test instrument had a high internal validity.

Table 5: Paired Samples Test

		Mean	Std. Deviation	Std. Error Mean	95% Confidence Interval of the Difference Lower	95% Confidence Interval of the Difference Upper	*t*	*df*	Sig. (2-tailed)
Pair 1	Total – total 2	2.200	11.841	5.295	12.502	16.902	.415	4	.699

Table 5 showed the *t*-test results. The significance = 0.699, which was greater than 0.05. Therefore, before and after scores were not different.

There was no intent to collect feedback as data, but to refine the instrument, vis-à-vis poorly worded questions, questions which may have caused confusion, questions that may have been ambiguous and/or repetitive, and to reveal the time required to complete the survey. Each panel member was contacted for a telephone interview to provide feedback regarding the following questions:

1. Were the survey directions easy to follow?
2. Are there statements or parts that should be added or deleted?
3. How did you feel about the length of time it took to complete the survey? Is the survey too long to be completed in one sitting?
4. Do you have any suggestions on how the survey instrument could be improved?

The results were used to refine and clarify the questions, and identify any potential problems (see Appendix B). Reliability is, "The degree to which the survey results are free from random error, as opposed to systematic bias, often expressed in terms of confidence intervals or confidence levels" (Alreck & Settle, 2004, p. 447). Therefore, the reliability of the survey instrument was demonstrated in the similarity of the first set of panel responses with the second set of panel responses, and was estimated by Pearson correlation to be not less than 90%.

The Survey Monkey electronic survey was also tested by this panel, specifically for timing. The panel felt the electronic survey was much more pleasant to take, and it took less time. The timing of the survey went from approximately 20 minutes, the time it took to complete the email version, to approximately 10 to 15 minutes, for the time it took to complete the electronic version.

Survey Administration

The human resource department at each organization distributed the cover letter with the Survey Monkey link via email. Human resource departments securely house electronic distribution lists for their employees and volunteers. At no time did the researcher have access to these distribution lists and, therefore, was not able to identify or directly contact individual respondents.

Respondents had two weeks to complete the survey and submit it electronically via Survey Monkey. Reminder e-mails were sent to participants via human resources for a second distribution, seven days after the initial e-mail with cover letter and the survey link.

When the survey closed, the data file was downloaded and the Survey Monkey account was closed. The data was secured by the researcher on a flash drive which was held in a locked security box throughout the analysis and until the publication processes were completed. All information was stored securely for three years, per Argosy University, Tampa requirements. At the end of the thee years, all recorded data and other information was deleted and all written data shredded. The data was destroyed after publication was finalized.

Statistical Tests

The level of statistical significance for this study was alpha $\leq.05$. P values were compared to alpha to determine the significance of the tests. Frequencies of all variables were used to create a profile of the respondents. Participants received an affiliation score used to predict purchase preference using linear regression. Linear regression was applicable since sample was not normal, and sample size was >25.

The Spearman correlation rank was an applicable measurement for this study because, "The Spearman rank-order correlation coefficient was a non-parametric measure of the strength and direction of association that exists between two variables measured on at least an ordinal scale. The test was used for either ordinal variables or for continuous data that has failed the assumptions necessary for conducting the Pearson's product-moment correlation" (Statistics.laerd.com). Spearman rank correlations between "affiliation" and "purchase preference" variables were compared to confirm the statistical significance and direction of associations found with linear regression models. Linear regression was appropriate, since the predictor variable, affiliation was a continuous variable, and since the sample size was greater than 25, the researcher was able apply the central limit theorem and assume the population was sufficiently normal.

Data Processing and Analysis

Only data from respondents who answered all questions needed to test the hypothesis were used for analysis to test the hypothesis. SPSS computer-based quantitative analysis software was used.

Obtain permission from IRB to proceed with survey	Send out email to HR contacts at organizations	On day seven, send reminder email to HR contact at organization	Total time to administer survey to respondents, 14 days

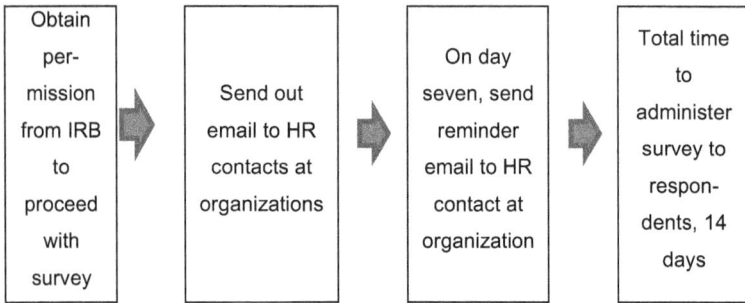

Figure 4 - The sequence of the research study events.

Numeric data was used to break down affiliation and purchase preference into groups of low, medium and high. According to Suhr (1999), "There are distinct differences between principal component analysis (PCA) and exploratory factor analysis (EFA)." The PCA was a variable reduction technique which will help to identify which preference or preferences were most important to respondents. The EFA was also a variable reduction technique which identified the number of latent constructs and the underlying structure of a set of variables" (p. 3).

The total amount of variance in PCA was equal to the number of observed variables being analyzed. In PCA, observed variables were standardized, e.g., mean=0, standard deviation=1, diagonals of the matrix were equal to 1. The amount of variance explained was equal to the trace of the matrix (sum of the diagonals of the decomposed correlation matrix). The number of components extracted was equal to the number of observed variables in the analysis. The first principal component identified accounts for most of the variance in the data. The second component identified accounts for the second largest amount of variance in the data and was uncorrelated with the first principal component. Components accounting for maximal variance were retained, while other components accounting for a trivial amount of variance were not retained. (Suhr, 1999, p. 2)

Assumptions Underlying Principal Component Analysis (PCA)

The five assumptions underlying Principal Component Analysis (PCA) were presented.

1. Interval-level measurement. Some of the measurements were on interval/ratio scales. For

example, the Likert ratings of likelihood to purchase certain CRM campaign products. Other measurements, such as being an employee of or having an immediate family member/close friend as an employee of a charity, was a nominal measurement as in "yes" or "no." It could not be said one was greater than the other.

2. Random Sampling. The sample is a convenience sample, but it was random and from the target population.

3. Linearity. It was expected the relationship between all the variables would be linear.

4. Normal distributions. It was expected each observed variable would have a normal distribution; the Shapiro-Wilks test was used to test this assumption.

5. Bivariate normal measurement. It was expected each pair of observed variables would have a bivariate normal distribution. However, the expected sample size was >25.

Principal Component Analysis was not used for this study, because normal distributions and bivariate normal measurement were not met. A Shapiro-Wilks test was conducted on outcome variables which revealed that some purchase preferences were not normally distributed. The distributions of the responses to likelihood to purchase a CRM product ($p = 0.006$), likelihood of making a CRM vs. non-CRM purchase ($p = 0.046$), and the importance of the charitable organization ($p = 0.009$) slightly deviated from normality. While the distributions of the responses to the importance ratings the product itself ($p = 0.179$), the CRM sponsor ($p = 0.834$), the CRM donation practice ($p = 0.881$) and the product's brand ($p = 0.052$) did not significantly deviate from normality.

Since this topic had not previously been explored, it was more relevant to the hypothesis to identify the structures that could be measured. Once more was known about this topic, latent constructs and underlying factors could be explored. Therefore, principal components analysis (PCA) of the response categories was not conducted.

CHAPTER FOUR:

RESULTS

Restatement of the Purpose

The purpose of this research study was to investigate the prevalence and strength of a consumer's affiliation with a charity, and to quantify the strength of the relationship between charity affiliation and consumer purchase preference for CRM campaign products.

Research Question

This study explored the following research question.

Research Question 1: What is the relationship between charity affiliation and purchase preference for cause-related marketing campaign products?

Research Findings

The online survey data collected was statistically analyzed using SPSS software. A demographic profile of the respondents was presented first, followed by the affiliation data and purchase preference data required to test the following hypothesis. The remainder of this chapter presents the analysis of additional survey data that added depth and breadth to the topic exploring respondents' thoughts on cause-related marketing, and greater depth concerning their volunteer experience and purchase preferences. Although not required to test the hypothesis, this additional data was of interest, but analyzed later in greater depth.

H_1: There is a relationship between charity affiliation and purchase preference for cause-related marketing campaign products.

H_0: There is not a relationship between charity affiliation and purchase preference for cause-related marketing campaign products.

Survey Response Data Analysis

Of the five organizations who participated in this study, three were for-profit organizations and two were non-profit charities. The survey instrument consisted of 47 questions and was administered online via Survey Monkey. Three hundred fifty-four completed and partially completed surveys were received, of which 333 were usable for testing the hypothesis. Twenty-one surveys were discarded because the respondent did not complete enough of the survey to be meaningful. Most of these discarded surveys had only answered the qualifying question. "Missing data reduces sample size and thus may threaten statistical power" (Langkamp, Lehman, & Lemeshow, 2010, p. 1).

Respondent Demographic Profile

Fifty-five (55.6%) percent of the respondents were female. The respondents' average age was 47.5 years. Baby Boomers were best represented at 42%; Generation X at 28%, Millennials/Generation Y at

26%. Most (84%) respondents were Caucasian.

Approximately 24% of respondents had earned a high school diploma. A bachelor's degree was earned by 35% of the respondents and 23.4% had earned a graduate degree (masters or doctorate).

Career status was segmented into employed (full or part time), retired (job or no job), career stage, in college and their educational or career goal. Percentage (7.29%) of respondents who were in college were becoming qualified to improve or change their current career, while 1.04% were in college qualifying for their first career. Respectively, 18.75%, 17.71% and 16.67% of participants were in their early, mid and late careers. In regard to career, 12.50% of participants were working in their second career, 10.42% were working part-time, 39.58% working full-time. While 2.08% of participants were stay at home parents, 6.25% were retired with a part-time job, 6.25% were retired with no job, and 3.13% were unemployed. Annual household income included 33.3% earning between $31,000 and $50,000; 49.8% earning $51,000 to $150,000; and 10.5% earning over $150,000.

Respondents' daily living situation revealed 22.64% lived alone, 53.77% lived with a spouse, 13.21% lived with a roommate, and 10.38% were living with a partner. Respondents reported living with up to four children (12.50% answered "1", 8.33% answered "2", 2.08% answered "3" and 1.04% answered "4") in their household on a regular basis, while most (76.4%) of respondents had no children in their homes, (median of 0 children).

Respondents lived in the Tampa Bay area, on average, 22 years whereas they averaged working in the Tampa Bay area for 16 years (see Table 6).

Table 6: Respondent Demographics

Demographic	n	Category	%	Mean
Gender	333			
		Female	55.6%	
		Male	44.4%	
Age	333	All		47.5 years
Generation	333			
		Gen Z (18)	27.6%	
		Gen Y / Millennials (19035)	26.4%	
		Gen X (36-51)	27.6%	
		Baby Boomer (52-70)	41.7%	
		Silent Generation (71+)	3.9%	

Demographic	n	Category	%	Mean
Race	333			
		White / Caucasian	84.4%	
		Black/African American	6.9%	
		Asian	3.6%	
		Other	5.1%	
Education	333			
		High School Diploma/GED	23.7%	
		Associates Degree	14.1%	
		Bachelor's Degree	35.4%	
		Master's Degree	18.3%	
		Doctorate Degree	5.1%	
		None of the above	3.3%	
Career Status	96			
		In college for first career	1.04%	
		In college for career change	7.29%	
		In my early career	18.75%	
		In my mid-career	17.71%	
		In my late career	16.67%	
		In my second career	12.50%	
		Working part time	10.42%	
		Working full time	39.58%	
		Full-time military	1.04%	
		Stay at home parent	2.08%	
		Retired with a part-time job	6.25%	
		Retired, no job	6.25%	
		Unemployed	3.13%	
Annual Household Income	333			
		$31,000-50,000	33.3%	
		$51,000-150,000	49.8%	
		>$150,000	10.5%	
Living Status	212			
		Living alone	22.64%	

Demographic	n	Category	%	Mean
		Living w/spouse	53.77%	
		Living w/roommate	13.21%	
		Living w/partner	10.38%	
Children Living Daily in the Home	96			
		No children	76.04%	
		1 Child	12.50%	
		2 Children	8.33%	
		3 Children	2.08%	
		4 Children	1.04%	
Tampa Bay Area	96			
		Living in Area		22 years
		Working in Area		16 years

Affiliation

Affiliation was, "An individual's relationship to a charity. The consumer and the consumer's immediate family members and close friends who at the time of the study or in the past were an employee of, a volunteer with, a beneficiary of, or a donor (product or money) to a charity" (Kuntz-Azan, 2016). For this study, affiliation was measured for both the respondent and the respondent's immediate family/close friends.

Respondent Affiliation

Respondents were asked six questions to measure affiliation used to test the hypothesis: one on employment, three on volunteering, one on donations, and one on benefitting. Respondent affiliation was measured utilizing the following six questions. The frequencies were reported below (see Table 7).

1. Currently working for a non-profit or for-profit organization (employment)
2. In the last month, how many hours have you volunteered at a charity (volunteering)
3. Of last 10 years, how many years did you volunteer at a charity (volunteering)
4. Best description of your volunteer commitment to a charity in the last year (volunteering)
5. Items regularly donated to a charity (donations)
6. Directly benefitting from a charity (benefitting)

Table 7: Respondent Affiliation

Affiliation	n = 333	Category	%	Mean
Affiliation – Employment Currently working for		Non-profit charity	7.4%	
		Non-profit, not a charity	10.8%	
		Government or military	9.9%	
		For-profit organization	31.5%	
		Self employed	9.9%	
		None of the above	16.7%	
Affiliation – Volunteering Hours volunteered in the last month at a charity		1 to 8 hours	20.1%	
		9 to 16 hours	6.9%	
		17 to 32 hours	2.7%	
		33 to 40 hours	0.3%	
		More than 40 hours	2.1%	
		Not volunteered	49.2%	
Number of years in last 10 years, volunteered at a charity		0 years	31.2%	
		1-3 years	16.8%	
		4-6 years	13.8%	
		7-10 years	18.6%	
				3.5 years
Volunteer commitment to a charity in the last year		At own convenience, no schedule	22.5%	
		Regularly scheduled, special events	6.3%	

Affiliation	n = 333	Category	%	Mean
		Regularly scheduled, weekly/monthly	4.8%	
		Both regularly scheduled, weekly/monthly and special events	8.1%	
		Not volunteered	39.6%	
Affiliation – Donating Regularly Donate		Money	48.9%	
		Food	35.1%	
		No regular donations	9.6%	
Affiliation – Directly Benefit		Yes, received benefits	18.3%	
		No, none received	63.1%	

Most (31.5%) respondents reported they worked for a for-profit organization. Some (10.8%) worked for non-profit organizations that were not charities, while others (7.4%) worked for non-profit charity organizations. The remainder worked for the government or military (9.9%) or were self-employed (9.9%). Approximately half (49.2%) of the respondents did not volunteer at a charity. Those who did volunteer, most frequently reported volunteering between 1 and 8 hours (20.1%). A few (2.1%) respondents reported volunteering for more than 40 hours 'the previous month.' The mean time spent volunteering during the last 10 years was 3.5 years and volunteering was typically (22.5%) done at the respondent's own convenience. Most respondents reported regularly donating clothing and household items; (18.3%) of the respondents reported they had directly benefitted from a charity.

Immediate Family/Close Friend Affiliation

Respondents were asked to recall their experience with and knowledge of their immediate family members and their close friends with respect to their affiliation with a charity. Respondents' immediate family/close friend's affiliation was measured with four questions used to test the hypothesis. The immediate family/close friend affiliation questions were as follows. Frequencies were reported below (see Table 8).

a. Currently or in the past been employed at a charity (employed)
b. Currently or in the past volunteered at a charity (volunteered)

c. Donated money, food, clothing and/or household items to a charity (donation)

d. Directly benefitted from a charity (benefitting)

Table 8: Immediate Family / Close Friend Affiliation

Affiliation (n = 333)	Category	%		
		Current	Past	Never
Currently / past employed at charity	Parents/Sibling	5.7%	6.3%	43.5%
	Spouse/Children	7.2%	4.5%	39.6%
	Close Friends	21.0%	5.1%	24.3%
Currently/past volunteered at charity	Parents/Sibling	20.4%	22.8%	11.1%
	Spouse/Children	20.1%	18.9%	12.9%
	Close Friends	36.3%	11.7%	4.5%
Clothing/Donations		Money	Food	House-hold
	Parents/Sibling	43.8%	33.6%	50.8%
	Spouse/Children	35.4%	30.9%	46.2%
	Close Friends	36.0%	33.6%	43.2%
Directly benefitted from charity (yes)	Parents/Sibling	44.1%		
	Spouse/Children	26.4%		

The respondents' close friends were more likely (21.0%) to currently[1] work at a charity and both

---

[1] *The term, 'currently,' when referenced in this publication, relates to the time period of this research study.*

(26.1%) currently and had, in the past, worked at a charity. Parent/siblings (12%) and spouse/children (11.7%) were very close in their working at a charity both currently or in the past.

Close friends were most likely (36.3%) to currently volunteer at a charity but least likely (11.7%) to have volunteered in the past. Whereas parents/siblings and spouse/children were equally (20%) likely to be currently volunteering.

The respondents' immediate family and close friends were most likely (over 43%) to donate clothing and household items, with monetary donations running a close second just over 35.4%. Over 30% of the respondents donated food. Close to half (44.1%) of the respondents had a parent/sibling and 26.4% had a spouse/children who had directly benefited from a charity.

The following table described the summary of affiliation. Maximum affiliation of respondent's score was 29.2, while the minimum was 1.4. Interestingly, each respondent had some type of affiliation with a charity (see Table 9).

Table 9: Summary of Affiliation

Affiliation scores	min - max	mean + SD
Benefit – Respondent	0 – 1	0.23 + 0.42
Affiliation – Respondent	1 – 20.2	7.95 + 4.74
Benefit – FF	0 – 2	0.87 + 0.51
Affiliation – FF	0 – 11	4.48 + 2.55
Benefit – total	0 – 3	1.09 + 0.71
Affiliation – total	1.4 – 29.2	12.42 + 6.40

Purchase Preference

Purchase preference was, "The choices made by consumers as to which products to consume" (Pass, Davies, & Lowes, 2006, p. 316). Respondents were asked two questions about their purchase preference for CRM products:

1. How likely are you to make a CRM purchase?
2. How likely are you to purchase a CRM campaign product rather than a non-CRM campaign product when the products are similar if not the same, the manufacturer is the same for both products, and the CRM donation practice is the same for both products?

Respondents answered the first question using a 7-point Likert scale starting with 1 – Not at all Likely, 4 – Neither Likely nor Unlikely, and ending with 7 – Very Likely. On this scale of increasing likelihood to make a CRM purchase, most respondents (27.0%) were neither likely nor unlikely to make a CRM purchase. However, respondents were less likely to answer "1, 2 or 3" (15.6%) than to answer "5, 6, or 7" (29%) suggesting more respondents were open to purchasing a CRM product than not (see Table 10).

Table 10: Likely to Make CRM Purchase

Likely to Make a CRM Purchase		%
Scale		
1	Not at all likely	9.9%
2		3.6%
3		2.1%
4	Neither likely nor unlikely	27.0%
5		13.2%
6		6.9%
7	Very Likely	9.6%

In the second question, respondents were asked how likely they were to purchase the CRM vs. a Non-CRM product. Respondents used a 7-point

Likert scale starting with 1 – Not at all Likely to Purchase, 4 – Neither Likely nor Unlikely to Purchase, ending with 7 – Very Likely to Purchase. An eighth answer was provided: 8 – Depends on the Charitable Organization (see Table 11).

On this scale of 1 to 7 indicating increasing likelihood to make a CRM vs a non-CRM purchase, almost a quarter of respondents (20.1 %) were neither likely nor unlikely to purchase a CRM vs non-CRM product. However, respondents were less likely to answer "1, 2 or 3: (11.4%) than to answer "5, 6, or 7" (30%) suggesting more respondents were open to purchasing a CRM product over a non-CRM product than not. Approximately 10% of participants indicated it would depend on the charitable organization. The mean likelihood of 4.60 and the median rating of 4 were calculated omitting the respondent's choice #8 - Depends on the charitable organization (see Table 11).

Table 11:- Likely to Purchase CRM vs. non-CRM Product

Likely to Make a CRM Purchase		%
Scale		
1	Not at all likely	8.4%
2		2.1%
3		0.9%
4	Neither likely nor unlikely	20.1%
5		8.4%
6		6.0%
7	Very Likely	15.6%

Hypothesis Testing

The following hypothesis was tested using linear regression analysis with charity affiliation (respondent and immediate family/close friends) and purchase preference data.

H_1: There is a relationship between charity affiliation and purchase preference for cause-related marketing campaign products.

H_0: There is not a relationship between charity affiliation and purchase preference for cause-related marketing campaign products.

Linear regression was appropriate to use for this research study for two reasons. First, the predictor variable, affiliation, was a continuous variable. Second, the sample size was greater than 25. Consequently, the central limit theorem was applied and the population assumed to be sufficiently normal.

Individual Question Regressions

The first analysis individually regressed each of the affiliation questions on each of the two purchase preference questions. Spearman rank correlations between "affiliation" and "purchase preference" variables were compared to confirm the statistical significance and direction of associations found with linear regression models. These analyses were to determine if any individual affiliation questions predicted the respondents' purchase preference in general (likely to purchase CRM) or when faced with a decision between a CRM product and a Non-CRM product. Another use of this test was to find if any of the questions were not related to the purchase preference questions and, therefore, could be eliminated from future testing. Findings were as follows.

Table 12: Regression Model: Benefit Predicting Purchase Preferences

Benefit Predictor	Likely to Purchase CRM		Likely to Purchase CRM vs. Non-CRM	
	Coefficient (95% Conf. Intv.)	P Value	Coefficient (95% Conf. Intv.) P Value	P Value
Respondent Benefit	.0352	0.190	0.529	0.097
	(-0.176 – 0.881)		(-0.097 – 1.155)	
Immediate Family / Close Friends Benefit	-0/058	0.802	-0.438	0.121
	(-.059 – 0.394)		(-0.992 – 0.116)	

In summary, neither respondents nor their immediate family/close friends who directly benefitted from a charity significantly predict a respondent's likelihood of making a CRM purchase nor likelihood of choosing a CRM product rather than a non-CRM product (Table 12). Therefore, the data for beneficiary will be removed from testing the hypothesis. All other affiliation questions were significantly related to both individual purchase preference questions.

This left the respondent composite affiliation variable (score) comprised of the respondent's employment at a charity, donations to a charity, and volunteering at a charity for use in testing the hypothesis. The composite affiliation score for the immediate family and close friends included employment, volunteering, and donating to be used in the remaining linear regression models. The composite purchase preference score will be not changed for future linear regression models used to test the hypothesis.

Hypothesis Testing Linear Regression Models

Tables 13, 14, and 15 depict the regression analyses used to test the hypothesis. Each linear regression model used composite affiliation variables which have omitted the 'beneficiary' data for both the respondent and the respondent's immediate family and close friends. Three regressions were accomplished with various predictors: (1) respondent affiliation (R); (2) immediate family and close friend affiliation (IMF/CF); and (3) the total of both respondent and immediate family and close friend affiliation (R + IMF/CF). This first set of regressions predict the purchase preference question of "how likely are you to purchase a CRM product?" (Table 13).

Table 13: Summary of Linear Regression Models: Composite Affiliation Predicting CRM Purchase

Composite Affiliation Predictors	Coefficient (95% Conf. Int.)	P Value
Respondent (R)	0.084 (0.038 – 0.130)	< 0.001
Immediate Family/Close Friends (IMF/CF)	0.146 (0.060 – 0.233)	0.001
R + IMF/CF	0.069 (0.035 – 0.103)	< 0.001

As indicated, all three regression models were significant at the .001 level. Consequently, each of the three models significantly predicts the likelihood of purchasing a CRM product.

The next set of three regression models again uses the composite affiliation variables less the beneficiary data to predict purchase preference.

However, the purchase preference question used in these regression models was the likelihood of purchasing a CRM product rather than a non-CRM product (see Table 14).

As shown, composite affiliation for the immediate family and close friends and the total of respondent affiliation and the immediate family and close friends regression were significant at the .005 level. Whereas the respondent affiliation was significant at the .05 level when predicting the likelihood of purchasing a CRM rather than a non-CRM product.

Table 14: Summary of Linear Regression Models: Composite Affiliation Predicting CRM vs. Non-CRM Purchase

Composite Affiliation Predictors	Coefficient (95% Conf. Int.)	P Value
Respondent (R)	0.072 (0.016 – 0.129)	0.013
Immediate Family/Close Friends (IMF/CF)	0.154 (0.049 – 0.258)	0.004
R + IMF/CF	0.064 (0.023 – 0.106)	0.003

Lastly, linear regression was used to predict the impact of composite affiliation variables (scores) on the composite purchase preference variable (score) (See Table 15). Again, beneficiary data had been omitted from the composite affiliation scores. Immediate family and close friend composite affiliation was the strongest predictor at the .05 significance level. Both composite respondent affiliation and the sum of respondent and immediate family and close friend composite affiliation were significant predictors of the composite purchase preference variable (score).

Table 15: Summary of Linear Regression Models: Affiliation Predicting the Composite Purchase Preference Score

Composite Affiliation Predictors	Coefficient (95% Conf. Int.)	P Value
Respondent (R)	0.111 (0.019 – 0.204)	0.018
Immediate Family/Close Friends (IMF/CF)	0.231 (0.060 – 0.403)	0.008
R + IMF/CF	0.098 (0.030 – 0.166)	0.005

Summary of Results

This exploratory study revealed fresh information about the new variable "charity affiliation" and its relationship to purchase preferences for CRM products. First, the definition of charity affiliation had been explored through individual affiliation question regressions on the two purchase preference questions (likelihood of purchasing a CRM product and likelihood of purchasing a CRM product rather than a non-CRM product). With the exception of being a beneficiary of a charity, all affiliation questions for employment, volunteering, and donating were significantly related to both purchase preference questions and the composite score for these questions. Being a beneficiary of a charity was not significantly related to purchase preferences (each individual question or the composite score). Therefore, the definition of charity affiliation should be updated to remove the "affiliation of being a beneficiary" for both the respondent and the respondent's immediate family and close friends.

Second, the hypothesis was supported using linear regression models with composite affiliation scores (respondent, immediate family and close friends, and the total of these composite scores) being used to predict purchase preferences (both individual questions and the composite score of the two questions). Those three models (nine regressions) clearly substantiated all affiliation predictors were significant by themselves and when combined and regressed on purchase preferences (both individual questions and the composite score).

Third, from the nine linear regressions used to test the hypothesis, it was found the largest impact on purchase preference was made by the affiliation of immediate family members and close friends. Respondent affiliation was second and total affiliation was third in impact on purchase preference.

Fourth, the linear regression models also supported a positive relationship between affiliation scores (respondent, immediate family and close friends, and the total of both) and purchase preference (each individual question and the composite of the two). In other words, as one affiliation score (independent variable) increased, the dependent variable of purchase preference also increased. This pattern was seen for all affiliation scores and all purchase preference scores. The statistical significance and direction of this association were similar to those found by conducting a Spearman rank correlation.

Overall, the findings from this research study contributed greatly to the academic marketing literature and, specifically, to cause related marking literature. This study serves as a foundation for future research and continued progress in the content area of cause-related marketing. The following hypothesis had statistical significance.

H_1: There is a relationship between charity affiliation and purchase preference for cause-related marketing campaign products.

Supplemental Statistical Analysis

As previously stated, the survey included additional questions not used in hypothesis testing. These questions contributed to a better understanding of the respondents' motivation and experience with charities and decision-making when presented with cause-related marketing campaigns. The survey instrument regarding those questions is protected under copyright. Please contact Dr. Carolanne Kuntz Azan at dr.carolannekuntz@yahoo.com, or Dr. Sherri Kae at sherrijk@gmail.com, for further information.

Summary of Supplemental Data

As previously stated, additional questions were included in the survey to provide greater depth to this study. These findings were interesting, but require further statistical analysis in addition to analyzing the additional data not presented here. These analyses were being completed, and the results will be forthcoming in a second book.

CHAPTER FIVE:

SUMMARY, RECOMMENDATIONS, AND CONCLUSION

Summary of Study

This chapter summarizes the previous chapters to include presenting the problem and purpose of the study, to review the literature and discuss the research findings, the limitations and delimitations and the implications and implementations for practice, as well as areas for future research. Contributions to the academic literature stream, and a conclusion of the findings from a statistical analysis of the data collected, were presented.

Statement of Problem

With recent economic downturns, charitable donations dwindled and grants went away. Charities are forced to fiercely compete for fewer remaining grants against many more applicants than ever before. More time and effort is put into searching for and attracting individual donors; however, with the financial well-being of donors devastated by the stock market crash, donor's money was also tight. The limited availability of and greater competition for financial grants, coupled with a reduction in contributions to charities, placed greater dependence on for-profit organizations with a CRM mission. Over the years, CRM has proven its value to for-profit organizations and supported the existence and growth of charities desperate for funding in the most recent of economic downturns. Consequently, improving the marketing and sales of CRM products is greatly needed to continue the good work provided by charities.

Purpose of Study

The purpose of this research study was to investigate the prevalence and strength of a consumer's affiliation with a charity, and to quantify the strength of the relationship between charity affiliation and consumer purchase preference for cause-related marketing campaign products.

Review of the Literature

The literature review consisted of five CRM themes. Opening with a discussion of corporate social responsibility (CSR) followed by CRM and CRM-marketing strategy and segmentation, and concluding with the characteristics of affiliation and purchase preference. These five themes were supported by synthesized information from the existing marketing literature.

Over the years, much of the academic research has turned to the nuances of CRM and provided insights into the strategies and CRM components related to such a strategy. Although other studies have investigated CRM from a variety of angles, this study explored consumer affiliations with charities and their purchase preference for products of CRM campaigns.

Current research indicates that, "Despite the increased use of charity linked promotions, few investigations have examined the factors that influence the effectiveness of CRM" (Strahilevitz & Myers, 1998, p. 434). Liston-Heyes and Liu (2013) stated, "While there is considerable work on CRM from a corporate angle, very little has been done from a non-profit perspective, particularly in terms of developing a conceptual and theoretical understanding of the strategies available to non-profit managers" (p. 1974).

Runte, Basil, and Deshpande (2009) concurred, "Very little research has addressed the impact of CRM on managerial issues relevant to non-profit organizations. Engagement of participants in the CRM process has been the focus of recent research, although considerable knowledge gaps remain" (p. 257). Taylor (2012) stated, "Further research is needed on relationships that are economic in nature for non-profit organizations, thereby filling a gap, or an apparent variable that has possibly been ignored, in the past" (p. 203). Taylor (2012) also suggested, "There is a need for research on market segmentation for identifying relationships that influence behaviors" (p. 10). Fornier (1998) explained, "Although the relationship metaphor dominates contemporary marketing thought and practice, surprisingly little empirical work has been conducted on relational phenomena in the consumer products domain, particularly at the level of the brand" (p. 343). This exploratory research study was designed to investigate the relationship between charitable affiliation of potential consumers and their purchase preferences for CRM campaign products.

Methodology

Quantitative research methods were used in this primary exploratory research to identify and evaluate the relationships between the independent variable of affiliation and the dependent variable of purchase preference. The sections of the survey instrument addressed demographics, affiliation and purchase preference. The instrument of measure for this study is the Charitable Affiliation and Consumer Purchase Preference for Cause-Related Marketing Campaign Products survey instrument. The exploratory nature of this study is best served by the survey instrument specifically developed for the study. To test reliability, the survey was initially administered to a panel of experts and the correlation determined by Pearson Correlation Coefficient, which maintained that reliability was not less than 90%.

The survey instrument consisted of 47 questions and was administered to the participants anonymously. The research was conducted via on-line collection of data. The sample of 333 completed surveys consisted of employees from three for-profit organizations, and employees and volunteers from two charitable non-profit organizations, all located in the Tampa Bay area. The data was analyzed and compared to the research question and related hypothesis.

Through statistical analysis, using the Spearman rank-order correlation coefficient, the null hypothesis was tested and it was found that affiliation was significantly related to some purchase preferences. A unit increase in individual affiliation caused an increase of 0.084 (p < 0.001) in the likelihood of making a CRM purchase. A unit increase in immediate family or close friend affiliation caused an increase of 0.146 (p = 0.001) in the likelihood of making a CRM purchase. Unit increase in individual affiliation caused an increase of 0.072 (p = 0.013) in the likelihood of making a CRM vs. a non-CRM purchase. A unit increase in immediate family or close friend affiliation caused an increase of 0.154 (p = 0.004) in the likelihood of making a CRM vs. a non-CRM purchase.

The importance of the charitable organization in a CRM campaign was influenced by affiliation. A unit increase in individual respondent affiliation caused an increase of 0.049 (p = 0.003) in the importance rating of the charitable organization in a CRM campaign. However, benefiting from a charity did not affect purchase preferences.

Findings

As in Chapter Four, the following hypothesis had statistical significance.

H_1: There is a relationship between charity affiliation and purchase preference for cause-related marketing campaign products.

Hypothesis testing revealed that respondent employment at a charity, donations to a charity and volunteering at a charity (measures of affiliation) were found to be significantly related to CRM purchase preference for both the likelihood of making a CRM purchase and likelihood of making a CRM vs. a Non-CRM purchase. Hypothesis testing also revealed immediate family members/close friend's affiliation was significantly related to CRM purchase preference for both the likelihood of making a CRM purchase and the likelihood of making a CRM vs. a Non-CRM purchase. Respondent affiliation and the immediate family members/close friend's affiliation together was significantly related to the composite CRM purchase preference score, which revealed that when individual affiliation increased, purchase preference increased. Thus, the alternative hypothesis indicated there is a presence of a relationship between affiliation and purchase preference, and is accepted.

Interestingly, being a beneficiary of a charity did not affect purchase preferences. Psychologically, benefiting from a charity may bring back embarrassing and uncomfortable feelings from a difficult time in the beneficiary's life. Typically, persons do not plan to be beneficiaries of a charity and in most cases, this was due to an unplanned event.

Limitations and Delimitations of Findings

The following limitations occurred when conducting the research. The survey consisted of 47 questions. All 333 respondents answered questions about demographics, charity affiliation and purchase preference, which were used to test the hypothesis. Demographic limitations include the geographic location of sample. This study was completed in the Tampa Bay area. It is not uncommon for generalizability to be a limitation of exploratory research such as this study. The convenience sample, geographic location of the respondents, type of charities, and sample size greatly impact generalizability. It is expected that the results are generalizable to the culture of other similarly structured organizations in the Tampa Bay area.

The survey's length impacted the respondents' completion of the survey which included skipping questions and simply stopping the survey early before finishing all the questions. Some respondents may have feared their managers would be able to see their answers. Others may have been interrupted during the survey or they tried to complete the survey within a defined time-period, such as a break at work. Respondents' concentration may have been hampered by their interest in the content or the activities surrounding them while taking the survey if at work or at home with family.

One of the for-profit organizations delayed distributing the survey by seven days. The researcher was notified via e-mail by the organization's human resource manager after the researcher sent the reminder e-mail. During the halfway date of the study, the response rate was low. The researcher noticed the respondents tended to stop at the ten-minute mark. Before re-sending the link to the aforementioned for-profit organization, the survey was reordered with the first section of demographics, affiliation, purchase preferences, and last section of demographics moved up. This was put into a new survey link and was sent to the aforementioned for-profit organization. Therefore, survey questions were reordered, the window for responding was shorter (seven days), and a reminder **was not sent to that** for-profit organization.

This was a last-minute decision made by researcher. Due to the circumstances with the organization and an evaluation of the pattern of incomplete surveys already received, it was decided re-ordering the survey questions would facilitate the submission of the completed questions supporting the testing of the hypothesis. Consequently, this change in question order was made to improve the response rate of the questions used to test the hypothesis.

Implications and Implementations for Practice

Charities, sponsors and consumers were all impacted by the results of this study. The implications and implementation of these findings are discussed for each group.

Charities. Most important, charities will pay more attention with whom they team with as a sponsor. Specifically, their contract with their sponsor, which includes donation practice, and when and how the funds will be paid, may impact the success of the CRM campaign and the number of donations the charity receives. The charities may also pay more attention to the appeal of the campaign product and the relationship of the product to the charity's mission and strategy. Charities may be required by sponsors to provide contact information to the sponsor for their volunteers, employees, and supporters for specialized market segmentation and campaign advertising purposes. Charities may attract new sponsors resulting in a better opportunity for increased donations or lose current sponsors thus reducing their CRM donations. Overall, charities will be paying more attention to their CRM campaign relationships and contracts, which should improve their reputation and donations. This may improve the success of the CRM campaign, the charity's reputation, and the number and amount of donations the charity receives. They may also be faced with asking employees and volunteers for permission to release their contact information for CRM campaigns when they are first on-boarded with the charity as a condition of their service.

A better understanding of charity affiliation will assist charities with relating highly affiliated and less affiliated consumers to their segmentation and targeting strategies. Charities could identify the less-involved consumers and determine the basis of their lack of involvement. Grau and Folse (2007) suggested, "From a strategic viewpoint, gaining the attention of less-involved consumers has important implications for non-profit organizations. These less-involved consumers may be the key to future effectiveness for CRM campaigns as competition among companies allying with causes increases" (p. 19).

Sponsors. Sponsors previously adopting a CRM campaign strategy to primarily improve their reputations and make their advertising more competitive may need to reconsider their strategy as a long-term move to improve profitability and improve the trust of their consumers in their organization and their products. A new strategy with respect to the adoption and implementation of a CRM campaign may result in sponsors reassessing their campaigns and re-evaluating the CRM components (sponsor, charity, product and donation practice) for problems and for the relationship of their current practices with a new strategy. This research suggests a new way to target markets that could assist with the creation of product lines that may be more appealing based on demographics. For example, the respondent profile in this study were middle aged, Caucasian females, on the Baby Boomer/Gen X cusp, living with a spouse, with some college education, working full-time and making between $50K and $150K.

This type of thorough evaluation may result in sponsors identifying mismatched CRM campaigns, products, charities or donation practices. Sponsors may choose to completely sever current CRM relationships or to reformulate their CRM campaign contracts with their charity partner.

The perception and reputation of charities may be more attractive to sponsors. CRM campaigns are about an effective strategy and higher profits for sponsors as well as being socially responsible and transparent in the eyes of the sponsor's consumers;

and doing what is most advantageous for the charity and increasing the sponsor's donation amount. The positive impact on the reputation for the sponsor will come as part of the CRM package.

Both charities and sponsors will want to adjust their market segmentation and targeting practices based on the findings of this research. This research suggests that CRM is extremely sensitive to demographics. A better understanding of purchase preference based upon the strength of consumers' affiliation may support or alter current market segmentation and the targeted marketing efforts of both CRM sponsors and charities engaged in CRM, or in their daily mission to find more volunteers and donors.

Consumers. This study suggests consumers want more transparency regarding the amount of the donation per product and the specific use of the funds by the charity. Greater transparency provides consumers with a basis to trust the sponsor and feel the value and impact of their donation when making a CRM purchase. Consumers felt good about donating clothing and household items, most likely because they knew the value of their donation and the potential value of their donation to the charity, again, a very transparent relationship. Improving the transparency of the CRM donation practice and the use of the campaign's donation to the charity should improve consumers' feeling for the value of their donation and the value felt by the charity.

Consumers will face better decision-making information when evaluating a CRM purchase if sponsors and charities both engage in more transparent activities and choices for CRM campaigns. Sponsors may evaluate consumer trust in the CRM campaign itself, the sponsor, or the charity to better segment the market on charity affiliation or better define their consumers. The sponsor may also adopt a strategy of transparency in other offerings (non-CRM) to their consumers.

Recommendations for Future Research

This exploratory study targeted a general population in the Tampa Bay area. As a result of this research, seven recommendations for future research are provided below:

First, this research study could be duplicated with a different geographic area or in another country. Such research may be important to regional sponsors and charities or those with international branches or divisions.

Second, examining generational differences will provide greater insight into generational CRM values, decision-making and purchase preferences. A more age diverse population could be targeted or specific generations could be targeted in this research.

Third, an investigation into various aspects of and the importance and effectiveness of different advertising modes by generation (retiring Baby Boomers, Generation X, Millennials, and Generation Z) may be beneficial for more effective and efficient advertising strategies. With the demographic changes taking place at the time of this research study, assessing each generation could be beneficial for both market segmentation and targeting as well as the selection of advertising modes.

Fourth, researchers may also want to distribute the survey through social media, as this may allow for survey respondents to be rewarded for forwarding the survey to their social networks, thus increasing the breadth and reach of the research. Additionally, coupon discounts or other methods attractive to Millennial and Generation Z respondents are easily used as an incentive upon completion of the survey via social media.

Fifth, this survey included a question on the consumer's interest in searching for more information about a CRM campaign prior to purchase. For future research, it is recommended more questions be asked concerning the types of research consumers do before seriously considering the purchase of a CRM product, thus profiling the types of consumers looking for more detailed information about CRM campaigns.

Sixth, donation amounts were investigated in this research, however, the price to donation amount relationship was not investigated. Consequently, the development of a scale or formula for a consumer's perceived donation amount relative to the price of the CRM product may be helpful in better selecting more appropriate donation practices.

Lastly, respondents in this research were asked how likely they were to purchase a CRM product. However, future researchers may consider developing a survey wherein respondents are presented a variety of actual campaigns that employ various combinations of sponsor, charity, product and donation practice. Respondents would then be asked to make decisions for how likely they are to make the purchase. These suggestions for future research would further the academic marketing literature stream.

Contributions to Academic Literature Stream

"Charity Affiliation," and the measurement for affiliation are new to the academic literature stream, and will provide greater specification in charitable relationships and affiliation.

Conclusions

This study explored the following research question: What is the relationship between charity affiliation and purchase preference for cause-related marketing campaign products? The tested hypothesis was found to be statistically significant.

H_1: There is a relationship between charity affiliation and purchase preference for cause-related marketing campaign products.

The affiliation of both respondent and immediate family and close friends is important in an individual's decision to purchase a CRM product; however, there are other factors that contribute to their decision that may be revealed from additional questions on the survey when that analysis takes place.

Sponsors and charities will find this study of interest in their search for better designed CRM campaigns to include market segmentation, targeting, additional survey research, advertising and greater transparency. This would also include sponsor selection, charity selection, type of donation practice, and the product characteristics. This study fills a gap in the academic marketing literature by providing more information about affiliation, and how affiliation is defined and measured, as well as its significant relationship to purchase preference.

Recommendations for future research include targeting a larger population and geographic area, examining purchase preferences by various ways people benefit from a charity, and examining CRM consumers by generations. Current demographic trends suggest that these constructs warrant further exploration and would contribute new information to the academic literature stream.

REFERENCES

Alreck P. & Settel, P. (2004). *The surey research handbook* (3rd ed.) New York: McGraw-Hill.

Al-Tabbaa, O., Gadd, K., & Ankrah, S. (2013). Excellence models in the non-profit context: Strategies for continuous improvement. *The International Journal of Quality & Reliability Management, 30*(5), 590-612. doi:http://dx.doi.org/10.1108/02656711311315521

Andreasen, A., & Kotler, P. (2008). *Strategic marketing for nonprofit organizations* (7th ed.). Delhi: Dorling Kindersly.

Anuar, M., Omar, K., & Mohamad, O. (2013). Does skepticism influence consumers intention to purchase cause-related products? *International Journal of Business and Social Science, 4*(5).

Arnett, D. B., German S. D., & Hunt, S. D. (2003). The identity salience model of relationship marketing success: The case of non-profit marketing. *Journal ofMarketing, 67*(2), 89-105.

Austin, J. (2003). Strategic alliances. *Stanford Social Innovation Review, 1*(2), 48-55.

Baby Boomers (2015). Retrieved from www.pewresearch.org

Baghi, I., & Gabrielli, V. (2013). Co-branded cause-related marketing campaigns: The importance of linking two strong brands. *International Review on Public and Non-Profit Marketing, 10*(1), 13-29. doi:http://dx.doi.org/10.1007/s12208-012-0086-0

Baghi, I., & Gabrielli, V. (2013). For-profit or non-profit brands: Which are more effective in a cause-related marketing programme? *Journal of Brand Management, 20*(3), 218-231.

Bang, H., Ross, S., & Reio, T. (2013*).* From motivation to organizational commitment of volunteers in non-profit sport organizations. *Journal of Management Development, 32*(1), 96-112.

Barber, N., Pei, J., Bishop, M., & Goodman, R. (2012). Measuring psychographics to assess purchase intention and willingness to pay. *The Journal of Consumer Marketing, 29*(4), 280-292.

Barbu, A. (2013). Eight contemporary trends in the market research industry. *Management & Marketing, 8*(3), 429-450.

Barnes, N. G. (1994). Cause-related marketing revisited: The effects of the United Way scandal. *American Business Review, 12*(2), 95.

Baruch, Y., & Sang, K. (2012). Predicting MBA graduates' donation behaviour to alma mater. *The Journal of Management Development*, 31(8), 808-825.

Bellett, G. (2010, December 10). Charities and non-profits still feel the pinch. *The Vancouver Sun*, 10A.

Bucic, T., Harris, J., & Arli, D. (2012). Ethical consumers among the Millennials: A cross-national study. *Journal of Business Ethics, 110*(1), 113-131 doi:http://dx.doi.org/10.1007/s10551-011-1151-z

Carby-Hall, J. (2005). Wherefore art thou the social responsibility of the enterprise? The United Kingdom experience. *Managerial Law, 47*(6), 205-234.

Castillo, M. (2015). Reflections on participatory budgeting in new york city. *The Innovation Journal, 20*(2), 2-11.

Chang C. 2012. The effectiveness of advertising that leverages sponsorship and cause-related marketing: a contingency model. *International Journal of Advertising, 31*(2): 317–337.

Choi N. G., & Kim, J. (2011). The effect of time volunteering and charitable donations in later life on psychological wellbeing. *Ageing and Society, 31*(4), 590-610. doi:http://dx.doi.org/10.1017/S0144686X10001224

Cohen, A. (1992). A power primer. *Psychological Bulletin, 112*(1), 155-159. http://search.proquest.com/docview/

Consent. Retrieved from http://dissertation.laerd.com/principles-of-research-ethics.php

Corcoran, B. (2015). School news. *Bangor Daily News*

Creswell, J. (2005). *Educational research: planning, conducting, and evaluating quantitative and qualitative research.* Upper Saddle River: Prentice-Hall.

Creswell, J., Klassen, Ann, Clark, Vicki, & smith, K. (2010). Best practices for mixed methods research in the health sciences. *The Office of Behavioral and Social Sciences Research (OBSSR) of the National Institutes of Health* (NIH), 1-39. https://obssr.od.nih.gov/scientific_areas/methodology/mixed_methods_research/pdf/Best_Practices_for_Mixed_Methods_Research.pdf

Deac, V., & Stanescu, A. (2014). Strategic segmentation - the preamble of developing a company strategy. *Revista De Management Comparat International, 15*(4), 461-469.

DeBard, R. (2004). Millennials coming to college. *New Directions for Student Services,* (106), 33-45.

Demetriou, M., Papasolomou, I., & Vrontis, D. (2010). Cause-related marketing: Building the corporate image while supporting worthwhile causes. *Journal of Brand Management, 17*(4), 266-278. doi:http://dx.doi.org/10.1057/bm.2009.9

DeMillo, R. (2006). Questionnaire Design. Georgia Institute of Technology Website. Retreived from http://www.cc.gatech.edu/classes/cs6751_97_/winter/Topics/quest-design

Dorfman, P. W., Gupta, V., Hanges, P. J., House, R., & Javidan, M. (2004). *Culture, leadership, and organizations-The GLOBE study of 62 societies.* California: Sage Publications, Inc.

Dupont, S., A.P.R. (2015). Move over millennials, here comes generation Z: Understanding the 'new realists' who are building the future. *Public Relations Tactics,22*(5), 19.

Eikenberry, A. (2013). A critical case study of cause-related marketing. *Administrative Theory & Praxis, 35*(2), 290-305.

Elfenbein, D. W., & McManus, B. (2010). A greater price for a greater good? evidence that consumers pay more for charity-linked products. *American Economic Journal.Economic Policy,2*(2), 28-60. doi:http://dx.doi.org/10.1257/pol.2.2.28

Folse, J., Niedrich, R., & Grau, S. (2010). Cause-relating marketing: The effects of purchase quantity and firm donation amount on consumer inferences and participation intentions. *Journal of Retailing, 86*(4), 295-309.

Forester, D. (2013). What is the difference between a nonprofit organization and a charity? Retrieved from http://www.score.org

Fournier, S. (1998). Consumers and their brands: Developing relationship theory in consumer research. *Oxford University Press, 24*(4), 343-353.

Foxall, G. (1978). Marketing response to consumer loyalty. *The Quarterly Review of Marketing, 3*(3), 6.

Franzak, F., Makarem, S., & Jae, H. (2014). Design benefits, emotional responses, and brand engagement. *The Journal of Product and Brand Management, 23*(1), 16-23.

doi:http://dx.doi.org/10.1108/JPBM-07-2013-0350

Furlow, N. (2011). Find us on facebook: How cause marketing has embraced social media. *Journal of Marketing Development and Competitiveness, 5*(6), 61-64.

Gibaldi, C. P. (2014). The changing trends of retirement: Baby boomers leading the charge. *Review of Business, 34*(1), 50-57.

Goldberg, M. (1995). Social marketing: Are we fiddling while Rome burns? *Journal of Consumer Psychology, 4*(4), 347-371.

Grau, S., & Folse, J. (2007). Cause-related marketing (CRM): The influence of donation proximity and message-framing cues on the less-involved consumer. *Journal of Advertising, 36*(4), 19-33.

Haggerty, J. (2013, Mar 18). Aging baby boomers plan to work well beyond retirement. *The Times-Tribune.*

Hofstede, G. (1991). *Cultures and organizations: Software of the mind.* London: McGraw-Hill.

Hulyk, T. (2015). Marketing to gen z: Uncovering a new world of social media influencers. *Franchising World, 47*(12), 32-32, 34.

Johnston, L. F. (2002). *Maximizing donor value: Key satisfaction drivers for major donors to nonprofit organizations.*

Kelley, B. (1991). Cause-related marketing: Doing well while doing good. *Sales and MarketingManagement, 143*(3), 60.

King, J. E. (2001). *The role of feelings in decision-making according to Bernard Lonergan* (Order No. 3004171). Available from ProQuest Dissertations & Theses Global. (251636682).

Kotler, P., & Armstrong, G. (2014). *Principles of marketing* (15th ed.). Upper Saddle River: Pearson.

Kotler, P. & Keller, K. (2012). *Marketing management* (14th ed.). Boston: Prentice Hall.

Kumar, V. (2000). *International marketing research.* New Jersey: Prentice-Hall, Inc.

Kwan, A. C., & Cotsomitis, J. A. (2004). Can consumer attitudes forecast household spending in the United States? Further evidence from the michigan survey of consumers. *Southern Economic Journal, 71*(1), 136-144.

Lamb, C., Hair, J., & McDaniel, C. (2013) *Marketing* (12th ed.). Mason: Cengage.

Langkamp, D. L., Lehman, A., & Lemeshow, S. (2010). Techniques for handling missing data in secondary analyses of large surveys. *Academic Pediatrics, 10*(3), 205-210.

Liston-Heyes, C., & Liu, G. (2013). A study of non-profit organizations in cause-related marketing. *European Journal of Marketing, 47*(11), 1954-1974.

Liu, G., & Ko, W. (2011). An analysis of cause-related marketing implementation strategies through social alliance: Partnership conditions and strategic objectives. *Journal of Business Ethics, 100*(2), 253-281. doi:http://dx.doi.org/10.1007/s10551-010-0679-7

Luo, X. (2005). A contingent perspective on the advantages of stores' strategic philanthropy for influencing consumer behavior. *Journal of Consumer Behavior, 4*(5), 390-401.

Mason, T. (2002, Jun 06). Marketing for a better world? *Marketing,* 11.

Millennials (2015). Retrieved from http://www.pewresearch.org

Mohr, L., Webb, D., & Harris, K. (2001). Do consumers expect companies to be socially responsible? The impact of corporate social responsibility on buying behavoir. *The Journal of Consumer Affairs, 35*(1), 45-72.

Monroe, K. (June 1974). The influence of price differences and brand familiarity on brand preferences. *Journal of Consumer Research, 3,* 42-49.

Moosmayer, D. C., & Fuljahn, A. (2013). Corporate motive and fit in cause-related marketing. *The Journal of Product and Brand Management, 22*(3), 200-207. doi:http://dx.doi.org/10.1108/JPBM-04-2012-0125

Nelson, G. (2015). Boomers create deep wells of donations & volunteers: Are you ready to receive? Retrieved from http://www.nonprofitquarterly.com

Nguyen, T. T. M. (2015). Altruistic or opportunistic: Consumer perception of cause related products. *Academy of Marketing Studies Journal, 19*(1), 177-196.

Oberg, C. N. (2011). The great recession's impact on children. *Maternal and Child Health Journal, 15*(5), 553-554. doi:http://dx.doi.org/10.1007/s10995-011-0807-8

Pass, C., Davies, L., & Lowes, B. (Eds.), *Collins Dictionary of Economics.* London, United Kingdom: Collins.

Perception. *The concise oxford english dictionary* (11th ed.). Oxford University Press, 2008.

Peters, G. (2014) The alpha and the omega of scale reliability and validity: Why and how to abandon Cronbach's alpha and the route towards more comprehensive assessment of scale quality. *Bulletin of the European Health Psychology*

Society, 16(2).

Peterson, K. (2009). *Examining the product (RED) campaign: Millennials' self-identity and perception of the cause-branding initiative* (Order No. 1462792). Available from ProQuest Central. (305004114).

Pracejus, J. W. & Olsen, D.G. (2002). The role of brand/cause fit in the effectiveness of cause-related marketing campaigns. *Journal of Business Research, 57,* 635-640.

Preferences. (2006). C. Pass, L. Davies, & B. Lowes (Eds.), *Collins dictionary of economics.* London, United Kingdom: Collins.

Rozensher, S. (2013). The growth of cause marketing: Past, current, and future trends. *Journal of Business & Economics Research (Online), 11*(4), 181.

Runte, M., Basil, D., & Deshpande, S. (2009). Cause-related marketing from the non-profit's perspective: Classifying goals and experienced outcomes. *Journal of Non-profit & Public Sector Marketing, 21,* 255-270.

Rifon, N., & Trimble, C. (2002). An update on consumer involvement with products and issues: Thirty years later. *American Marketing Association. Conference Proceedings,* 13, 271-277.

Robson, M. J., & Mark A.J. Dunk. (1999). Case study developing a pan-european co-marketing alliance: The case of BP-mobil. *International Marketing Review, 16*(3), 216-230.

Sekaran, U. (2003). *Research methods for business: A skill building approach* (4th ed.). New York: John Wiley & Sons, Inc.

Serban, C., Iconaru, C., & Perju, A. (2012). Modeling Romanian consumers' behavior case study: Cause-related marketing campaigns. *Research Journal of Recent Sciences, 1*(10), 27-32.

Sherraden, M. S., Lough, B., & McBride, A. M. (2008). Effects of international volunteering and service: Individual and institutional predictors. *Voluntas, 19*(4), 395-421.

Shu-Pei, Tsai. (2009). Modeling strategic management for cause-related marketing. *Marketing Intelligence & Planning, 27*(5), 649-665. doi:http://dx.doi.org/10.1108/02634500910977872

Silverthorne, C. (2009-2010). Practicing universal management. *Industrial Management, 51*(1), 8-8-13, 5.

Smith, A. (1863). *An inquiry into the nature and causes of the wealth of nations.* Edinburgh: Adam and Charles Black.

Smith, S. & Alcorn, D. (Summer 1991). Cause marketing: A new direction in the marketing of corporate social responsibility. *Journal of Consumer Marketing, 8,* 19-35.

Spearman's Rank-Order Correlation. (2016). Retrieved from www.statistics.laerd.com.

Steinberg, W. 2011. *Statistics alive!* (2nd ed.). Los Angeles: Sage.

Strahilevitz, M., & Myers, J. (1998). Donations to charity as purchase incentives: How well they work may depend on what you are trying to sell. *Journal of Consumer Research, 24*(4), 434-446.

Strauss, J. , & Frost, R. (2014). *E-marketing* (7th ed.). Upper Saddle River: Pearson.

Szyckman, L., Bloom, P., & Blazing, J. (2004). Does corporate sponsorship of a socially-oriented message make a difference? An investigation of the effects of sponsorship identity on responses to an anti-drinking and driving message. *Journal of Consumer Psychology, 14*(1&2), 13-20.

Taylor, J. A. (2012). Relational exchange in non-profits: The role of identity saliency and relationship satisfaction. (Order No. 3531594, Old Dominion University). ProQuest Dissertations and Theses, 203.

The Corporate Social Responsibility Index Study (2010). Retrieved from http://www.bcccc.net/pdf/CSRIReport2010.pdf

Thompson, A. A., Strickland, A. J., & Gamble, J. (2007). *Crafting and executing strategy: Text and readings.* Boston, MA: McGraw-Hill/Irwin.

Thomas, M. L. (2007). *Cause-related marketing partnerships: An application of associative learning theory principles for both short and long-term success for the brand* (Order No. 3291648). Available from ProQuest Central. (304810533).

Thomas, M. L., Fraedrich, J. P., & Mullen, L. G. (2011). Successful cause-related marketing partnering as a means to aligning corporate and philanthropic goals: An empirical study. *Academy of Marketing Studies Journal, 15*(2), 113-132.

Thomas, V. (2005). Cause-related marketing: Bringing together senior organizations and businesses. *Generations, 28*(4), 71-74.

Tonkiss, F., and Passey, A. (2001). Trust, confidence and voluntary organizations: Between values and institutions.

Sociology, 33(2), 251.

Vallerand, R. J. (2012). From motivation to passion: In search of the motivational processes involved in a meaningful life. *Canadian Psychology, 53*(1), 42-52.

Vanhamme, J., Lindgreen, A., Reast, J., & van Popering, N. (2012). To do well by doing good: Improving corporate image through cause-related marketing. *Journal of Business Ethics, 109*(3), 259-274. doi:http://dx.doi.org/10.1007/s10551-011-1134-0

Varadarajan, P. R., & Menon, A. (July 1988). Cause-related marketing: a co-alignment of marketing strategy and corporate philanthropy. *Journal of Marketing, 52*, 58-74.

Wang, Y. (2014). Individualism/collectivism, charitable giving, and cuase related marketing: A comparison of Chinese and Americans. *International Journal of Nonprofit and Voluntary Sector Marketing, 19*, 40-51.

Webb, D. J., & Mohr, L. A. (1998). A typology of consumer responses to cause-related marketing: From skeptics to socially concerned. *Journal of Public Policy & Marketing, 17*(2), 226-238.

APPENDICES

APPENDIX A

SURVEY INSTRUMENT

The survey instrument used in this research was developed by Carolanne Kuntz Azan, DBA and Sheryl J. Kae, PhD., and is protected under copyright. Please contact Dr. Carolanne Kuntz Azan at dr.carolannekuntz@yahoo.com, or Dr. Sherri Kae at sherrijk@gmail.com, for further information.

APPENDIX B

Survey Instrument Feedback from Panel of Experts

- "I felt the survey was very user friendly, and the questions were easy to answer." The explanation of CRM and the examples were very helpful."
- The survey seems to repeat the word "campaign" a lot. You use the wording CRM campaign sponsor, and CRM campaign product. I found that to be distracting. Think about this when you do your editing, and see if "CRM sponsor" or "CRM product" will work just as well. I feel this will read better."
- I would add self-employed to Charitable Experience section, #1.
- "I found the survey to be interesting, because I am very involved in the community, and I am looking forward to your findings. Can any colors or pictures be added to the on-line survey to stimulate the respondent, or to make taking the survey more interesting for them?"
- "I am a devout Catholic, and I am familiar with one of

the sponsors mentioned in the survey, and promoting the selling of aborted fetuses for medical research. I am opposed to this, so I have very negative feelings about this sponsor. Is there any way you can add a place for comments? I feel that I would like to elaborate on some of my answers."

- "There is a question 12 (h) under guiding principles/personal rules that has more than one part to it. I found this difficult to answer. Could you rewrite that question, or break it down into four separate questions?"
- "I did not feel the survey was too long, but I have had experience with using Survey Monkey. They have an option where you can put only one or two questions on a page. I suggest doing that, so the respondent feels as if they are moving along, quickly."
- "Have you thought about using emoji's for some of the answers?"
- "The paper email survey took me 20 minutes to take."
- "The paper email survey took me 23 minutes to take."
- "The paper email survey took me 25 minutes to take."
- "The paper email survey took me 15 minutes to take."
- "The paper email survey took me 20 minutes to take."
- "People do not like it when they feel like they are being tricked. Question 12, letters o and z, may make some people a little uncomfortable, if they are not careful

about how they read them."

- "Recheck your CRM product question. You ask about the CRM charity in the question, but all the responses are about the CRM product."

- "The Survey Monkey survey was much quicker to do. It took me 11 minutes.

- "The Survey Monkey survey went a lot faster. It took me about 10 minutes."

- "The Survey Monkey survey took me 13 minutes."

- "The Survey Monkey survey seemed to go very fast. I timed myself at 13 minutes."

- "The Survey Monkey survey took me 15 minutes to do. It was more pleasant than the paper version."

INDEX

advertising 26, 59, 76, 79, 91, 93, 96, 102, 105, 107, 111, 226, 227, 231, 234, 238

affiliation .11, 12, 13, 21, 23, 25, 26, 33, 34, 35, 36, 39, 41, 42, 49, 66, 93, 110, 111, 113, 119, 121, 122, 131, 140, 142, 143, 144, 145, 146, 147, 148, 149, 150, 152, 153, 154, 157, 159, 160, 163, 167, 169, 173, 180, 181, 182, 187, 188, 193, 194, 195, 196, 197, 198, 199, 200, 203, 204, 205, 206, 207, 208, 209, 210, 211, 212, 217, 219, 220, 221, 222, 223, 225, 227, 229, 230, 233, 234

alliance partner................60

ALS Association 18, 59, 168

altruism........................128

altruistic attitudes...128, 138

American Express16, 54, 56

American Red Cross
   ARC............................... 82

ANOVA analysis............152

Anti-Defamation League.58, 59

ARC
   American Red Cross 82

ASPCA.........................109

Baby Boomer100, 102, 191, 228

Baby Boomers....22, 76, 93, 99, 100, 101, 102, 104, 118, 155, 189, 231, 237

Barnes & Noble 58, 59

beliefs......................86, 104

beneficiary 33, 36, 42, 64, 110, 111, 122, 143, 148, 159, 160, 163, 167, 193, 205, 206, 207, 209, 210, 223

board of directors 82

BOGO
   buy one get one free 79

boycotts 84

brand alliances 127

brand engagement .31, 132, 239

brand loyalty 30, 76, 108

brands 27, 31, 65, 66, 84, 102, 127, 131, 132, 133, 139, 237, 239

breach of contract lawsuits 84

bribery 82

Bureau of Labor Statistics 115

campaign product.....25, 26, 27, 29, 44, 46, 54, 58, 61, 75, 78, 79, 81, 90, 101,

112, 119, 122, 129, 130, 131, 134, 135, 136, 137, 139, 144, 161, 163, 167, 168, 169, 200, 226, 249
campaign products ...11, 26, 28, 32, 33, 34, 41, 49, 67, 68, 75, 76, 92, 93, 97, 98, 100, 101, 107, 110, 111, 113, 129, 134, 137, 140, 142, 143, 144, 145, 146, 148, 149, 157, 163, 167, 169, 173, 184, 187, 188, 203, 212, 217, 219, 222, 233, 234
campaigns 12, 17, 18, 31, 32, 40, 41, 44, 47, 50, 53, 54, 56, 57, 59, 60, 61, 65, 67, 68, 72, 75, 77, 78, 83, 90, 93, 94, 95, 97, 101, 106, 107, 110, 111, 114, 126, 127, 128, 130, 132, 135, 136, 137, 138, 139, 140, 143, 144, 158, 163, 167, 173, 213, 218, 227, 228, 230, 232, 233, 234, 237, 242
Cause-Related Marketing
    CRM . 2, 11, 13, 14, 43, 44, 45, 47, 54, 66, 77, 89, 167, 220
cell phone apps 110
central collection sites40, 69
charitable activities 94
charitable-giving behavior29
charities ..10, 11, 13, 16, 17, 22, 23, 24, 28, 35, 39, 40, 41, 50, 53, 57, 61, 64, 69, 71, 72, 74, 85, 90, 93, 95, 101, 103, 104, 108, 110, 111, 112, 113, 114, 118, 120, 122, 123, 146, 147, 148, 150, 151, 153, 155, 160, 163, 167, 170, 189,

196, 212, 216, 218, 223, 226, 227, 228, 229, 230, 231, 234
charity.....11, 13, 16, 19, 21, 23, 26, 27, 32, 33, 34, 38, 42, 43, 44, 45, 48, 49, 54, 56, 57, 58, 59, 60, 61, 62, 64, 65, 66, 68, 72, 75, 76, 77, 78, 79, 80, 82, 83, 90, 94, 95, 98, 111, 112, 113, 114, 116, 117, 118, 119, 121, 122, 127, 129, 130, 131, 134, 137, 139, 140, 141, 144, 145, 146, 147, 148, 149, 153, 155, 157, 159, 160, 162, 163, 167, 168, 173, 184, 187, 188, 193, 194, 195, 196, 197, 198, 199, 203, 205, 206, 210, 212, 217, 218, 221, 222, 223, 226, 227, 228, 229, 230, 233, 234, 235, 239, 243, 251
Charity Affiliation 11, 14, 43, 233, 278
charity-linked products 77
charity-linked promotions
   129
collaboration continuum ..65
collectivism 87, 244
competition ...40, 69, 71, 97, 216, 227
composite purchase
    preference variable....209
conflict of interest 83
consumer affiliation ..13, 33, 34, 110
consumer attitudes ...52, 95, 127, 130, 133, 137, 240
consumer behavior ...17, 29, 59, 67, 241
consumer brand bonds.132, 133

consumer decision process
..........................32, 97, 98
Consumer rewards 54
consumer skepticism.......19
consumer traits....41, 85, 89
consumer trust.........80, 230
consumer's affiliation 13, 33,
    112, 187, 217
consumer's confidence..168
consumers....12, 17, 19, 20,
    23, 25, 26, 28, 29, 31, 32,
    33, 41, 46, 50, 51, 52, 53,
    54, 56, 61, 65, 68, 74, 75,
    76, 77, 78, 81, 87, 90, 91,
    92, 93, 94, 95, 96, 98,
    102, 105, 106, 107, 108,
    109, 110, 111, 125, 126,
    127, 129, 130, 131, 132,
    133, 135, 136, 138, 139,
    140, 142, 150, 161, 162,
    200, 219, 225, 227, 228,
    229, 230, 232, 235, 237,
    238, 239, 240, 241, 242
convenience sample.......35,
    153, 170, 184, 223
corporate angle25, 141, 218
corporate social
    responsibility
    *CSR 15, 18, 19, 49, 51, 53,
    217, 241, 243*
Corporate Social
    Responsibility Index
    Study 18, 52, 243
corruption 81, 82
Cottonelle 75
CRM
    *Cause-Related Marketing
    .. 11, 12, 13, 14, 15, 16,
    17, 18, 19, 20, 21, 23,
    24, 25, 26, 27, 28, 29,
    30, 31, 32, 33, 38, 39,
    40, 41, 43, 44, 45, 46,
    47, 49, 50, 53, 54, 55,
    56, 57, 58, 59, 60, 61,*

    *62, 63, 64, 65, 66, 67,
    68, 69, 72, 73, 74, 75,
    76, 77, 78, 79, 80, 81,
    82, 83, 85, 87,88, 89,
    90, 91, 92, 93, 94, 95,
    96, 97, 98, 100, 101,
    105, 106, 107, 108,
    110, 111, 112, 113,
    114, 119, 122, 125,
    126, 127, 128, 129,
    130, 131, 132, 133,
    134, 135, 136, 137,
    138, 139, 140, 141,
    142, 143, 144, 145,
    146, 148, 157, 158,
    161, 162, 163, 167,
    168, 169, 173, 184,
    185, 200, 201, 202,
    203, 204, 205, 207,
    208, 210, 216, 217,
    218, 219, 221, 222,
    226, 227, 228, 229,
    230, 231, 232, 234,
    235, 240, 249, 251*
Cronbach's alpha...174, 241
cross-cultural setting 87
CSR
    *corporate social
    responsibility15, 31, 44,
    51, 52, 53, 69, 136, 217*
cultural differences 86
cultural dimensions..........86
cultural mindset 86
Cumberland Farms...18, 59,
    168
data collection 13, 35, 37,
    38, 144, 169, 171
Dave Thomas Foundation
    for Adoption ...18, 59, 168
deception 81
delimitations 38, 215
demographic niches 140,
    163
demographic trends.......235

demographics.....11, 12, 92, 140, 143, 157, 163, 173, 219, 223, 224, 228, 229
digital world 105
Direct Relief.......18, 59, 167
discretionary income 95, 99, 101
disposable income.........101
donation intent.................82
donation practice 29, 45, 59, 60, 77, 78, 80, 96, 138, 161, 167, 168, 185, 200, 226, 228, 230, 233, 234
donations 13, 16, 17, 24, 39, 40, 53, 55, 57, 67, 71, 72, 79, 83, 114, 117, 119, 123, 129, 143, 163, 194, 196, 206, 216, 222, 226, 238, 241
Donors.............29, 119, 122
Dress for Success ...73, 278
economic exchange 130, 134
economic transaction 95, 130, 135
economic trends 31, 135
emotional connection 102
emotional decision...24, 136
emotional trigger......24, 136
ethical dilemma 85
exploratory research.......35, 142, 170, 219, 223
external contracts 91
Facebook...............108, 133
family members ..14, 36, 42, 43, 147, 148, 158, 160, 173, 193, 197, 211, 222
Feed My Starving Children 106
financial risk.....................89
for-profit ..37, 40, 50, 61, 67, 69, 72, 84, 112, 150, 162, 170, 189, 194, 196, 224

for-profit organizations....13, 35, 37, 40, 67, 72, 153, 154, 170, 171, 216, 220
Fortune 500 57
fraud 82
fund raising
fund-raising 17, 43, 55, 161
fundraising...72, 74, 77, 280
generalizability..35, 36, 144, 169, 170, 223
generation 23, 51, 92, 98, 100, 101, 102, 105, 106, 231, 239
Generation Z ..99, 105, 106, 107, 110, 231, 232
Girl Scout......................162
global business...............86
global environment..........24
government funding..39, 71, 72
gratification 94
Great Recession..39, 40, 71
Guiding Principles, Personal Rules 167
Hershey's 59, 75
HIV/AIDS 58
household spending31, 135, 240
human interactions 29
Hurricane Katrina 82
identity saliency 28, 121, 243
individualism 87
Instagram 106, 108, 133
intangible attributes ...25, 26
Integrative Stage 65
Internal Revenue Service
IRS *69*
Kay Jewelers 18, 59
Kentucky Fried Chicken ..62
key indicators 89
key-customer segments140, 162

less-involved consumers 97, 227

limitation 35, 36, 170, 223

linear regression analysis 203

linear regression models .... See , See , See , See , See , See , See

Linking 24, 129, 132, 133

Macy's 109

market environment.........85

market segmentation 12, 21, 23, 33, 41, 89, 90, 91, 92, 107, 131, 142, 219, 226, 229, 231, 234

market segmenting..........32

market segments 21, 47, 90, 91, 98

market share 19, 96

market type.....................32

marketers26, 30, 32, 92, 98, 99, 100, 105, 106, 109, 136, 140, 162

marketing campaign .13, 43, 45, 161

marketing plan 25, 28, 29

marketing strategy 24, 30, 32, 49, 57, 82, 85, 89, 98, 217, 244

Millennial 103, 104, 105, 110, 232

Millennials...22, 93, 99, 102, 103, 104, 107, 156, 189, 191, 231, 238, 239, 241, 242

mixed-methods research .38

monetary 199

monetary donations 128

money.....15, 22, 23, 31, 33, 39, 42, 43, 45, 70, 72, 86, 96, 100, 111, 114, 117, 118, 119, 122, 129, 135, 159, 160, 193, 198, 216

moral dilemmas 85

motivator.........................27

motives 19, 53, 95

mutually beneficial non-profit organizations 16

Nabisco 59, 75

New Balance 18, 59, 109, 168

non-profit 10, 16, 17, 23, 25, 35, 37, 40, 66, 68, 69, 70, 73, 74, 84, 85, 97, 103, 114, 119, 127, 131, 135, 141, 150, 153, 170, 171, 173, 189, 194, 196, 218, 220, 227, 237, 241, 242, 278

nonprofits.........................16

Oprah Winfrey Leadership Academy Foundation..18, 59

partner brands 127, 132

patterns of assumptions ..86

Pearson correlation175, 178

Pearson Correlation Coefficient..................220

pensions 22, 100

perceptions ...18, 31, 52, 59, 86, 87, 135, 138

performance .16, 18, 43, 52, 55, 85, 127, 161

Philanthropic Stage 65

Pinterest 108

political leaders...............86

political risk......................89

positive motivational attribution.....................29

power consumers 105

pricing .80, 93, 97, 101, 144, 163

Proctor and Gamble 108

product costs 137

Product Red 58

professional alliances 86

profitability 19, 21, 51, 67, 96, 227
promotional activities .93, 97
psychographic questions 140, 164
psychological effects28, 117
public embarrassment 84
public images 18
Purchase Preference 11, 12, 13, 14, 21, 24, 25, 32, 33, 34, 38, 41, 46, 49, 97, 110, 112, 131, 132, 140, 143, 144, 145, 146, 148, 149, 157, 161, 162, 163, 164, 169, 173, 180, 181, 182, 187, 188, 200, 203, 204, 206, 207, 209, 210, 211, 212, 217, 218, 219, 220, 222, 223, 229, 233, 234
purchase preferences.....32, 142, 148, 152, 167, 185, 188, 210, 211, 219, 220, 221, 223, 225, 231, 235
purchasing behavior 32, 136
purchasing power 15, 31, 100, 101, 102, 104, 107, 135
QR
Quick Response 106
quantitative 9, 13, 34, 35, 38, 145, 146, 169, 181, 238
Quick Response
QR106
relational phenomena ... 142, 219
relationship marketing 90, 237
reliability .35, 145, 173, 174, 175, 176, 178, 220, 241
research study 33, 35, 93, 142, 144, 146, 150, 153, 154, 159, 169, 171, 182, 187, 204, 212, 217, 219, 231
role models ...116, 118, 121, 147, 160
rules and regulations 86
sales marketing method ..32
sales volume 137
sample size 35, 37, 150, 152, 170, 171, 180, 181, 184, 189, 204, 223
scandal 81, 83, 238
segmentation 20, 26, 28, 49, 89, 90, 91, 93, 107, 110, 111, 217, 227, 229, 239
segment-specific marketing plans 90, 91
sensitivity analysis .128, 138
social awareness 107
Social bonds 29
social cause ..43, 56, 57, 81, 102, 108
social exchange theory..117
social investment 17, 111
social media2, 92, 106, 107, 109, 110, 133, 231, 240
social responsibility ..31, 51, 52, 126, 238
Social Security.........22, 100
socially conscious consumers 132
socially responsible ..15, 17, 18, 51, 52, 53, 54, 95, 228, 241
socio-emotional 119, 130, 135
spending traits 30, 31, 76
sponsors .11, 17, 21, 24, 25, 33, 41, 45, 53, 57, 61, 64, 66, 67, 68, 69, 72, 74, 81, 85, 90, 93, 95, 107, 110, 111, 114, 225, 226, 228, 229, 230, 231, 250

SPSS 145, 181, 188
St. Jude Research
    Children's Hospital. 18, 59
Starbucks 18, 59
statistical analysis...36, 152,
    213, 215, 220
Statue of Liberty .. 16, 55, 56
stock market crash ...39, 40,
    70, 71, 216
strategic planning 30
streaming video 106
Super Bowl 108
survey administration 36,
    144, 146, 170
survey instrument 9, 37,
    144, 157, 166, 172, 173,
    178, 189, 219, 220, 247
Survey Monkey 37, 169,
    172, 178, 179, 189, 250,
    251
Susan B. Komen 58
Susan G. Komen Breast
    Cancer Foundation 62
Susan G. Komen
    Foundation..... 18, 59, 168
Tampa Bay .35, 38, 47, 139,
    150, 153, 157, 164, 165,
    170, 173, 191, 193, 220,
    223, 230, 278
Target 20, 47, 108
target audience behavior. 23
Target marketing 20
target markets 11, 25, 41,
    67, 131, 228
targeted marketing efforts
    .... 12, 33, 229
targeting
    target marketing 12, 21, 89,
      90, 92, 101, 105, 107,
      131, 227, 229, 231, 234

targeting practices ... 12, 229
tax-deductible 16
tax-exempt status 16
The United Way.............. 83
theft 82
themes.....................49, 217
TOMS Shoes 106
transactional model 57
Transactional Stage 65
transparency. 106, 229, 230,
    234
trends ... 18, 31, 53, 86, 135,
    238, 240, 242
Tweets
    Twitter.......................... *133*
Twitter....................106, 108
Unilever 18, 59, 167
upper management 82
US Department of Labor115
validity 35, 36, 132, 133,
    145, 170, 176, 241
Vine 106
Visa 59
volunteer.22, 33, 36, 38, 42,
    43, 94, 104, 110, 111,
    113, 115, 116, 117, 118,
    121, 122, 153, 159, 160,
    173, 188, 193, 194, 196,
    199, 278
volunteerism 114
Walmart 108
Wendy's....... 18, 59, 75, 168
World Wildlife Fund 59
Worldwide Fund for Nature
    82
Yoplait Yogurt............ 18, 59
YouTube 133

CURRICULUM VITAE

Carolanne Kuntz Azan, D.B.A.
Tampa, Florida
dr.carolannekuntz@yahoo.com

TEACHING PHILOSOPHY

We are currently experiencing rapid changes in business and marketing. I truly feel I have a responsibility to my students to keep up with these changes by continuing my own education, forming strong business networks and sharing those connections with my students. I do this by working closely with local organizations, inviting invigorating guest speakers into the classroom, and by encouraging field trips. Current trends must be incorporated into the curriculum, and courses should be revised continuously to meet objectives and to reflect the real-word business environment in the most up-to-date and practical ways.

Consequently, gone are the days of 90-minute lecture halls. I break my classes into interactive and organized sequences which exhilarate the students and make learning fun. Learning is applied with a focus on involving all students, individually and in team settings to stimulate functional conflict, creativity and innovative thinking. This can be done on line as well as on ground by carefully designing assignments and projects that stretch their personal vision of themselves and the world.

Hence, teaching is all about relationships. It is about total transparency and sharing who I am with my students, and valuing their time and energy and who they are as individuals. It is about working as a team to help my students achieve their goals and dreams. It is about intellectual connection and being able to transfer knowledge and experience to my students who are from varying generations in today's stimulating and diverse global classroom.

Therefore, I hope my students feel comfortable in approaching me with questions and/or when they need advice, or just to kindle intellectual conversation. I hope for this trusting bond while they are my students, and long after graduation!

PROFESSIONAL TEACHING EXPERIENCE

08/14 – Present, Adjunct Professor
Business/Marketing
Cumberland University, Lebanon, TN

- Responsible for teaching course content and presenting learning materials via online platforms through one to two courses per 8-week semester, to approximately 80 students. Constant communication with students, via text, phone, on line platform, e mail, Skype and FaceTime. Kept students interested and excited about weekly assignments, and reported attendance and grades in a timely manner.
- Updated courses to Canvas software platform.
- Virtual classroom was identified as best-practice and used for teacher training
- Incorporated higher-level learning and assisted students to develop information literacy and problem-solving skills

Courses taught:

- **Business and Society** – Study of management framework, emphasizing social and ethical responsibilities of business to both external and internal stakeholders.

- **Marketing Management** – Study of marketing decision process. Marketing opportunities are identified. Marketing programs and cross-functional implementation steps are developed in relation to various environments and organizational mission. Internal organizational relations and controls complete the study.
- **Principles of Marketing** – Study of marketing concepts from a managerial perspective; marketing mix of product, place, promotion, and price; institutions involved in marketing process are included for consumer and industrial goods and services; ethics
- **Organizational Structure and Behavior** – Study of organizational behavioral processes including motivation, leadership, decision making, and communication; and behavioral consequences such as group conflict, politics, change, and development.
- **Project Management** – Examines organization, planning, and controlling of projects and provides practical knowledge on managing project scope, schedule, and resources. Topics include project life cycle, work breakdown structure, and Gantt charts, network diagrams, scheduling techniques, and resource allocation decisions.

08/11 – 11/13, Lead Professor
Keiser University, School of Business, Tampa, FL

- Developed syllabi and materials for classes to align with academic and accreditation compliance; designed capstone courses, working one-on-one with business student(s)
- Taught to ~40 students per eight-week semester, in four-hour long classes via face-to-face platforms; counseled students outside class hours
- Coordinated business program to align with university's academic goals

- Assisted Dean of Academics with planning and organizing focus groups of CEOs to design curriculum for new programs; performed community outreach; formed relationships with local business owners as members of the advisory board; implement feedback and experience into business course curriculum
- Academic Advisor to >100 business and interdisciplinary studies students each semester; served as Acting Program Director in this role, over a period of two-years
- Implemented first student chapter of Rotaract, and guided 10 student leaders through the process and seating of student board positions
- Provided SME consulting as Co-Chair and lead faculty member for University Advisory Board Committee for accreditation standards; grew College of Business Advisory Board by over 60%, with relevant members providing industry feedback and advice
- Teamed with Office of the Chancellor to plan and execute the Grand Opening of the Tampa campus
- Planned and organized *Social Networking in Today's Market* and *LinkedIn* workshops for faculty, student, staff, and community
- Teamed with Office of the Chancellor for development of video contracts with local key business professionals to assist the marketing department to film commercials to promote new programs for the University; commercials launched in 2013 and 2014, to advertise, brand and build new technology programs

Courses taught:

- **Entrepreneurship** – Introduces development of business and the role of an entrepreneur in today's economy. Topics include general theories, principles, concepts and practices of entrepreneurship. Heavy emphasis is placed on lectures, readings, case studies and group projects.

- **Human Resource Management** – Presents current theories and research regarding the development of individual managers and business organizations. Cases illustrating developmental methods are utilized.
- **Recruitment, Selection and Staffing** – Techniques of analyzing the effectiveness and appropriateness of various instruments used by professionals. Students are introduced to the strategies associated with the use of different recruitment and selection techniques.
- **Labor Relations** – Includes collective bargaining, workplace diversity, human resources, unions and the National Labor Relations Act.
- **Performance Management** - Focuses on procedures in personnel psychology. Topics include selection, performance appraisal devices, job analyses, evaluations, calculation of reliability, validity of cutoff scores, needs assessments for training and theories of job assessment.
- **Leadership** – Introduces leadership, research perspectives on leadership, the personal side of leadership, the leader as a relationship builder, and the leader as a social architect.
- **Managing Diversity** – Addresses work experiences as it varies with gender and ethnic background in the USA; work-related stereotypes and attitudes, discrimination and harassment, career choice, occupational segregation, employment patterns, group differences related to fair testing / employment practices, relationship of diversity to processes, e.g., supervision, leadership, mentoring, power.
- **Operations Management** – Introduces fundamentals of operations management in manufacturing and non-manufacturing sectors; product and process design, demand forecasting, facilities layout and location, materials management, inventory management, production planning and quality assurance.
- **Business Ethics** – Applies an ethical dimension to business decisions in today's complex political, social, economic and technological environment.

- **Principles of Management** – Presents current and traditional views of management organized around a functional and process approach. Topics include basic management principles and theory and analysis of management functions in planning, organizing, staffing, directing and controlling.
- **Introduction to Marketing** – Principles and functions of marketing and role in a business environment. Utilization of guiding principles of relationship building to establish and maintain trust and confidence in products and/or services.
- **Introduction to Management and Organizational Behavior** – Introduces managerial principles including planning, organizing, staffing and control techniques; behavioral science formulation of individual needs, motivation and group processes utilized.
- **Project Management** – Importance of project management and teaches students to differentiate between product and project management; roles and responsibilities of a project manager, project environment and developing a quality project team, five steps of a project, construction of a network diagram and mathematics analysis techniques such as CPM and PERT.
- **Integrated Studies Capstone Course** – Requires students to demonstrate knowledge learned throughout the program and apply knowledge to real-world issues. Synthesize and integrate learning experiences acquired throughout program and to evaluate research and current topics relative to area of concentration.

PROFESSIONAL CAREER EXPERIENCE

03/17 – present, Curriculum Subject Matter Expert – Marketing Sales Management
Rasmussen College, Tampa, FL

- Implemented higher-level Associate and Bachelor marketing degree curriculum to program

- Utilized expertise in Bloom's Taxonomy in designing program curriculum courses, including: course descriptions, course vision, course analysis, course competencies, course learning objectives, course assessment designs, alignment to external standards
- Review and provide feedback to other Curriculum SMEs to enhance individual courses in the program; provide feedback on curriculum-related questions throughout program design process
- Subject Matter Expertise consulting include: Sales Management, Team Building (recruiting, selecting, orienting, and training employees), Meeting sales goals (negotiation, selling for customer needs, motivation of sales teams, sales planning, coaching, relationship building, market knowledge, and budgeting development), Forecasting and Buyer Behavior, Professional Selling, and Business Negotiation
- Teamed with Management/Marketing Program Director in recruiting both local and national marketing professionals for 2017 advisory board membership, resulting in a relevant and valuable team of marketing professionals for feedback on new degree programs

**03/17, Curriculum Summit, Subject Matter Expert –
Marketing Sales Management
Rasmussen College, Bloomington, MN**

- Attended and participated in the three-day, in-person summit at a Rasmussen College campus located in Minnesota; collaborated and utilized expertise in Bloom's Taxonomy in creating: program vision, student learning outcomes, program alignment to external standards, alignment to institutional transferable skills, and course list with a draft of course competencies for marketing courses

08/08 – 05/10, Associate Director
University Outreach and Business Development
Argosy University, Tampa, FL

- Built relationships and partnerships with business community, educators, potential students and potential employers for graduates
- Implemented and oversaw operations for completing articulation agreements
- Coordinated and hosted open-house and transfer-day events
- Planned / scheduled lead-generating events, networking opportunities, oral presentations, and sponsorship opportunities throughout Florida.
- Responsible for a $30K campus marketing budget
- Finished first fiscal year as #1 BDR (Business Development Rep) in activity and lead production
- Formed relationship with St. Petersburg College (SPC) to coordinate Doctoral Program at Argosy to become a part of SPC University Alliance
- Established articulation agreements between Argosy and Hillsborough Community College (HCC)
- Initiated articulation agreement process at St. Petersburg College and Pasco Hernando Community College
- Developed School of Business Graduate Professional Workshop events in Business Etiquette
- Built relationships through networking, cold calling, fundraising and chamber memberships, which helped grow and promote Argosy University's branding

05/08 – 09/08 Reader/Scorer
Management Incorporated, Tampa, FL

- Performed nationwide academic writing and performance assessment examinations during a temporary summer project; finished in top 10 percentile for production and accuracy for nation's largest provider of writing and performance assessment

- Continued project work with a team of the Top 20 Readers/Scorers on special assignment, assessing future persuasive writing topics; assisted in meeting deadlines on projects

11/98 – 06/05, Associate Trust Administrator / Branch Manager
SunTrust Bank, Tampa, FL

- Reorganized and managed a branch not meeting sales goals; procured largest personal trust account in region's history
- Supervised and directed 10 tellers and private bankers, assessed and conducted bi-annual performance reviews
- Responsible for business development and client retention; created, planned, and hosted promotional events.
- Coordinated weekly sales meetings with visual sales charts; updated daily reports for end-of-day meetings, and met deadlines; created new promotions and visual lobby displays
- Increased profits and productivity in customer retention, personal/business banking, private lending, and investments; led branch onto leader boards in all categories; became benchmark branch for regional goals
- Developed customer interview technique that became the 'best practice' regional standard for training branch employees; interactive tactics expanded banking opportunities with business clients, resulting in increased productivity and banking sales relationships
- Performed recruiting for sales, banker, teller positions

03/93 – 04/98, Marketing Associate
Raymond James & Associates, Holiday, FL

- Assisted branch manager with sales, marketing, public relations and administrative tasks

- Specialized in account transfers and the funding of new accounts; handled branch public relations with the local media, utilizing compliance department rules and regulations; communicated with clients face-to-face, via telephone and e-mail
- Designed a telemarketing area; wrote and designed monthly newsletter; planned and hosted branch activities, events, and seminars
- Recruited, interviewed, and hired marketing assistants and telemarketers for financial advisors; supervised 10 telemarketers and mentored for weekly goal setting; trained telemarketers and mentored financial advisors
- Solved account transfer concerns with establishment of multi-million dollar accounts (east coast branch)
- Coordinated bi-annual fund-manager seminars, and hosted high-net-worth clients on private tours at the New York Stock Exchange.

FORMAL EDUCATIONAL DEGREES

**2016, Doctor of Business Administration
Argosy University, Tampa, FL**

Relevant Courses:

- Global and Multinational Marketing
- Selected Marketing Topics
- Conflict Management
- Marketing and Innovation
- Independent Study in Marketing
- Consumer Decision & Behavior
- Leading Innovation and Change
- Corporate Social Responsibility
- Solutions Leadership
- Managing Global Challenges
- Solution-Oriented Decisions Models
- Strategic Planning and Implementation

- Advanced Academic Study and Writing
- Introduction to Research Methods
- Methods & Analysis of Qualitative Research
- Methods and Analysis of Quantitative Research
- Survey Techniques
- Comprehensive Examination
- Dissertation

2001, Masters Degree in Business Administration, Major: Management
Nova Southeastern University, Fort Lauderdale, FL

Relevant Courses:

- 21st Century Management
- Law/Ethics
- Managing Technology & Information Systems
- Delivering Superior Customer Value
- Managing Organizational Behavior
- Managing Human Resources
- Quantitative Thinking
- Economic Thinking
- Accounting for Decision Making
- Managerial Marketing
- Applying Managerial Finance
- Entrepreneurship & Strategic Thinking
- Operations & Systems Management
- Leadership & Values Management

1999, Bachelor of Arts
Major: Organizational Management
Warner Southern College, Lake Wales, FL

Relevant Courses:
- Principles of Marketing
- Organizational Behavior Management
- Human Resources Management
- Managerial Finance

- Systems/Operations Management
- Knowledge Management

PROFESSIONAL TRAINING

Cumberland University

- Course development using Canvas, 2017

Keiser University, Tampa, FL

- Professional Development and In-Service Training, 2011-2013
- Completed on-line training courses and Blackboard, 2013
- Annual Convocation, 2011-2013

Argosy University, Atlanta, GA

- Business Development Training, 2008.
- Public Speaking and Presentations, 2008

Sun Trust Bank, Atlanta, GA

- Successfully completed Management Training Program in Private Wealth Management and Trust Administration with various continuing education courses between 2000 and 2005.
- Professional Etiquette Training Course, 2000.

Sun Trust Bank, Tampa, FL

- Private Banker and Teller Training, 1998
- Compliance Training, 1998
- Bank Security Training, 1998
- Various banking, investment and insurance courses between 1998 and 1999

Raymond James University, St. Petersburg, FL

- Compliance Training, 1993
- Financial Securities Training, 1993
- Various training courses in sales, marketing, finance and administration between 3/01/93 and 4/01/98

PUBLICATIONS

Kuntz Azan, C. (2017). *Charity Affiliation: Uncovering a Key Variable for Cause-Related Marketing.* Virginia Beach/Richmond, VA: DBC Publishing.
Kuntz Azan, C. (2016). *Charity Affiliation and Consumer Purchase Preference for Cause-Related Marketing Campaign Products. (Dissertation)* ProQuest Database.

CONTRIBUTIONS TO LITERATURE / RESEARCH ACTIVITIES

- Definition of Charity Affiliation: "An individual's relationship to a charity. The consumer and the consumer's immediate family members and close friends who currently or in the past were an employee of, a volunteer with, or a donor (product or money) to a charity" (Kuntz-Azan, 2016).
- My research has filled a gap in the cause-related marketing literature by defining charity affiliation and linking it to the purchase preferences of consumers of CRM products.
- Measurement of Charity Affiliation – Designed survey instrument to measure Charity Affiliation. The survey is protected by Copyright, 2016.
- Baby Boomer, Gen X, Gen Y, and Gen Z Purchase Preference for Cause-Related Marketing Donation Practices and Components

- Determining significant relationships between charity affiliation and consumer purchase preference for CRM campaign products, specifically within the roles of donors and volunteers.

EDUCATIONAL COMMITTEE CONTRIBUTIONS

- 2016 – present, Rasmussen College School of Business Advisory Board Member
- 2011- 2013, Founder, Charter, Rotaract student membership, Keiser University
- 2011 – 2013, Faculty Advisor/Mentor, Rotaract, Keiser University
- 2011 – 2013, Co-Chair, Advisory Board Committee, Keiser University
- 2011 – 2013, Chair, Business Administration Advisory Board, Keiser University
- 2012, Tampa Campus Coordinator, Campus Grand Opening Celebration, Keiser University
- 2008 – 2010, Member, School of Education Advisory Board, Argosy University
- 2008 – 2010, Member / University Representative, Tampa Bay Higher Education Alliance, Argosy University

COMMUNITY INVOLVEMENT

- 2012 – present, Member, Rotary Club, New Tampa, FL
- 2009, Fund Raiser, Leukemia and Lymphoma Association of the Suncoast, Tampa, FL
- 2008 – 2013, Greater Tampa Chamber of Commerce, Tampa, FL
- 2006 – 2011, Mentor, Take Stock in Children, Hillsborough Education Foundation, Tampa, FL
- 2006, Fund Raiser, Bark in the Park Walkathon, Tampa Bay Humane Society, Tampa, FL

- 1993 – 1998, Fund Raiser, Walkathon, United Way, Holiday, FL and Melbourne, FL

HONORARY / PROFESSIONAL ASSOCIATIONS

- 2015 – present, Member, American Marketing Association, Tampa, FL
- 2014 – present, Member, Sigma Beta Delta, International Honor Society in Business, Management and Administration, Tampa, FL
- 2012 – 2013, Society of Emotional Intelligence, Tampa, FL
- 2012 – 2013, Tampa Bay Technology Forum, Tampa, FL

HONORS AND AWARDS

- 2017, Finalist for American Marketing Association, Tampa Bay 2016 Marketer of the Year. Category: Marketing Research, Tampa, FL
- 2017, Finalist for American Marketing Association Tampa Bay Marketer of the Year. Category: Student
- 2017, Finalist for the American Marketing Association Marketer of the Year. Category: Overall Marketer of the Year
- 2013, Recipient, Distinguished Employee of the Year Award, Keiser University, Tampa, FL
- 2013, Finalist, Business Woman of the Year in Education, Tampa Bay Business Journal, Tampa Bay, FL
- 2012, Finalist, Business Woman of the Year in Education, Tampa Bay Business Journal, Tampa Bay, FL
- 2009, Finalist, Woman of the Year, Leukemia & Lymphoma Society, FL

AUTHOR BIO

Dr. Carolanne Kuntz Azan, known to her students and colleagues as 'Dr. Kuntz,' grew up on Long Island, New York, and has resided in Florida since 1986. She completed her undergraduate work at St. Petersburg College with an Associate Degree in Office Systems Technology, and at Warner Southern University, with a Bachelor's Degree in Organizational Management. She graduated with a Masters of Business Administration from Nova Southeastern University, and a Doctorate in Business Administration, with a concentration in Marketing, from Argosy University. She is an active member of Sigma Beta Delta International Honor Society in Business, Management and Administration, New Tampa Rotary and the American Marketing Association.

Her professional background includes teaching business and marketing courses on-line and on-ground, developing higher-level course content for marketing courses, trust administration, investments, retail and commercial banking and marketing. Her areas of specialization are cause-related marketing, management, and wealth management. With a deep passion for mentoring her students both inside the classroom and out, Dr. Kuntz formed the initial charter and the first Rotaract Chapter at Keiser University. Dr. Kuntz was a finalist for the American Marketing Association's Tampa Bay 2016 Marketer of the Year. She was also a finalist for the Tampa Bay Business Journal's 'Business Woman of the Year in Education' in both 2012 and 2013. She has contributed to the academic literature stream with the definition and measurement of Charity Affiliation.

Her greatest passions are charitable non-profit organizations that focus on education and pet rescue. She spent many years as a volunteer mentor with the Hillsborough Education Foundation's *Take Stock in Children* program, and she served as an after-school math and reading tutor to elementary school children in Title I schools. She is a supporter of Metropolitan Ministries, Dress for Success, the USO, Guiding Eyes for the Blind, and pet rescue missions in Tampa and St. Augustine, FL. Dr. Kuntz enjoys spending her free time in St. Augustine, with her husband and their four rescue pets.

CONNECT TO THE AUTHOR

LinkedIn: LinkedIn.com/in/carolanne-kuntz-azan-dba

Twitter: @carolanneazan

Email: dr.carolannekuntz@yahoo.com

Contact the author directly for any interest in partnership for the following research subjects:

- Baby Boomer, Gen X, Gen Y, and Gen Z Purchase Preference for Cause-Related Marketing Donation Practices and Components.

- Determining significant relationships between charity affiliation and consumer purchase preference for CRM campaign products, specifically the roles of donors and volunteers.

BOOK REVIEWS

In this book, Dr. Kuntz is able to explore the deeper subtleties of *Cause-Related Marketing* as a business competitive advantage and in doing so has taken steps to move marketing efforts into a more humanistic endeavor, a key ingredient for a globally competitive environment.
~ *Dr. Ronald R. Rojas, PRISM Leadership Consulting Group*

Dr. Kuntz does an outstanding job explaining the many factors impacting non-profit fundraising and how it affects the charitable organization as a whole. Personally, I have been active in animal rescue for over 20 years. Dr. Kuntz's innovative strategies offer readers new ideas to create a win-win outcome for all parties involved.
~ Melissa A. Sweeney, DBA, Author *of Love from Luke: Lessons Learned from a Rescued Dog*

Dr. Kuntz's research forges a new branch in the Cause-Related Marketing (CRM) literature by defining charity affiliation and linking it to the purchase preferences of consumers of CRM products. No longer can we do what we have always done for the sponsor's product when strategically partnering with a charity; we must tailor marketing strategies to the supporting community of the charity, and the market's support of the charity.
~ *Sherri Kae, Ph.D., Kaeberry Consulting*

ABOUT THE BOOK

The research conducted for this book indicates the presence of a relationship between *charity affiliation* and consumer purchase preference for Cause-Related Marketing (CRM) campaign products. A better understanding of purchase preference based upon the strength of consumers' affiliation could support or alter current market segmentation and the targeted marketing efforts of both CRM sponsors and charities engaged in CRM.

This research suggests a new way to target markets that could assist with the creation of CRM product lines which may be more appealing to consumers. Challenging the traditional market segmentation of CRM products suggests a newer and stronger viewpoint of development and implementation of a CRM strategy to achieve the best outcomes for *both* for-profit business sponsors and non-profit charities. Marketers at both for-profit and non-profit organizations, and consumers could all be positively impacted by the results of this exploratory research.

www.ingramcontent.com/pod-product-compliance
Lightning Source LLC
Chambersburg PA
CBHW060334200326
41519CB00011BA/1934